How to support children learning

English *as an*
additional language

Chris Pim

Acknowlegements

I should like to thank the following colleagues for advice and support on specific parts of the book. Without their generous time this book would never have been written.

Firstly, my deepest thanks to Sue Lee, with whom I had many interesting discussions that helped clarify and shape the content, for all her help in planning the major elements of the book. Thanks also to Sue Lee and Anwen Foy for quality assuring the first draft.

I am also indebted to a whole range of schools and colleagues who offered guidance and insights for specific elements of the book. These include the following: Yvonne Wilkin (Cummins Framework), Rajani Arora (assessing pupils' progress and English as an additional language), Smita Neupane (sourcing and contextualising Nepali writing sample), Nicola Davies (assessment and 1:1 tuition), Debbie Loveridge (Mathematics Family Learning Workshop), Astrid Gouwy (Hampshire Young Interpreter Scheme); also children and staff at St Mark's Church of England Junior School, Southampton; and St Bernadette's Catholic Primary School, Farnborough.

Permission to photocopy

This book contains materials which may be reproduced by photocopier or other means for use by the purchaser. The permission is granted on the understanding that these copies will be used within the educational establishment of the purchaser. The book and all its contents remain copyright. Copies may be made without reference to the publisher or the licensing scheme for the making of photocopies operated by the Publishers' Licensing Agency.

The right of Chris Pim to be identified as the author of this work has been asserted by him in accordance with sections 77 and 78 of the Copyright, Designs and Patents Act 1988.

How to support children learning English as an additional language
106640
ISBN-13: 978 1 85503 488 4

© Chris Pim
Cover illustration © Robin Edmonds
Inside illustrations © Garry Davies
All rights reserved
First published 2010
Reprinted 2010, 2011, 2013, 2014

Printed in the UK for LDA
LDA, Findel Education, Hyde Buildings, Ashton Road, Hyde, Cheshire, SK14 4SH

Contents

Introduction

As I took my first tentative steps towards writing this book, I imagined the feelings that an early-stage pupil learning English as an additional language (EAL) might experience as they nervously attempted their first English composition and I reflected on how threatening it was to confront the blankness of that piece of paper. Moving out of my comfort zone felt uncomfortable and I needed some strategies to help me in this new endeavour.

Initially I spent a lot of time just thinking about my new undertaking. After that it helped to talk with friends and colleagues, particularly in the relaxed atmosphere of my own home. As we were all in the same area of work, we were able to communicate in a common language, a lingua franca, which helped us overcome easily the many nuances of educational jargon and pedagogy. It was very useful to make lots of notes and to play around with different formats for presenting information. I certainly felt I was making progress once I had determined the basic structure as I could see more easily where to place the different pieces of information. At the beginning I found it quite difficult to write informally as I was more used to an academic style of writing. Looking at other books in the 'How to' series helped model the style for me. Regular feedback on content, style and layout from an editor helped focus my attention on specific elements that required some redrafting.

What struck me about the whole process is that no matter who we are, when confronted with a new learning context we all require strategies to support us in achieving our goals.

My experience highlights a number of common themes in supporting EAL learners that will be visited over and over again throughout the course of this book. Here are some of these:

- ◗ safe and secure setting
- ◗ importance of oracy as a springboard to literacy
- ◗ use of a preferred language in which to learn
- ◗ drawing upon prior knowledge and skills
- ◗ working collaboratively in small groups
- ◗ modelling the use of informal/formal writing
- ◗ scaffolding learning by using writing frames and graphic organisers
- ◗ constructive and informative feedback – assessment for learning (AfL).

Who is this book for?

Primary-phase practitioners, including:

- governors with specific responsibility for inclusion

- senior leaders / key staff with a specific focus on raising ethnic minority achievement (EMA)

- all staff working with pupils learning EAL

- student teachers working towards qualified teacher status.

What this book hopes to achieve

Here is something for you to bear in mind. It permeates the pages of this book:

That which is good for EAL pupils is good for all pupils.

However, while good practice for EMA is most certainly about quality-first teaching, this book aims to articulate the message that there is something very distinctive about the needs of EAL learners and to offer a range of practical ideas and strategies to support this area of work.

Its specific aims are:

- to dispel the many myths surrounding effective provision for pupils learning EAL

- to identify whole-school approaches for raising EMA

- to draw on research about bilingualism to inform best practice within the classroom for beginner and advanced bilingual learners

- to consider the full range of appropriate and targeted interventions for EAL learners

- to establish how provision for race equality and promotion of cultural diversity makes a positive contribution to the whole school community.

Definitions

Minority ethnic / Ethnic minority

Everyone has an ethnicity and this ethnicity is self defined. This could be based on common ancestry, memories of a shared past, a shared cultural identity which might include kinship, religion, language, shared territory, nationality or physical appearance. (http://www. standards.dfes.gov.uk/ethnicminorities/raising_achievement/whats_new/ terminology/) Groups that are significantly under-represented compared to the national population may be described as being in the minority. As a useful working definition, 'minority ethnic' refers to anyone with a declared ethnic background who is not white British.

Bilingual

In England the term is currently used to refer to pupils who live in two languages, who have access to, or need to use, two or more languages at home and at school. It does not mean that they have fluency in both languages or that they are competent and literate in both languages. (D. Hall et al. 2001, p. 5)

Monolingual

Some minority ethnic pupils born in the UK have grown up in households where they have not been exposed to other languages. This description is principally about languages that might influence a learner from an early age.

EAL

English as an Additional Language is the expression used in the UK to refer to the teaching of English to speakers of other languages (http://www.multiverse. ac.uk/ViewArticle2.aspx?Keyword=Eal&SearchOptio n=Phrase&SearchType=Keyword&RefineExpand=1& ContentId=381) These are individuals nurtured from birth in another language. English has been acquired subsequently.

Non-EAL

Individuals who have been nurtured from birth in English. Other languages have been learned subsequently.

Beginner

A beginner EAL learner might be described as someone who has yet to develop competence in everyday spoken English and is at a beginning stage of learning reading and writing. Such learners tend to be relatively newly arrived in the UK.

Advanced

An advanced EAL learner tends to be fairly secure in colloquial oral language. However, they have not yet developed full academic proficiency in speaking, listening, reading and writing across the curriculum.

Food for thought
All EAL children are bilingual, but not all bilingual children are learning EAL.

Chapter 1
What do we know about our EAL learners?

Pupils learning EAL are not a homogeneous group. They are no more similar to each other, on average, than any other pupils in a particular category are to each other. It would be a mistake to assume that EAL learners are all the same. That is simply untrue, and it could encourage the attitude that they should all be treated the same. This chapter aims to demonstrate the complex lives and experiences of EAL learners, whether UK born or recently arrived from abroad. In particular, it touches upon what the research says about the best practice and principles for supporting all our EAL learners.

Maslow's hierarchy of needs

The psychologist Abraham Maslow (1908–70) had the view that we all have levels of needs that must be met in order for us to function as fully integrated human beings. In the composite scenario below, a modified example of his hierarchy of needs, a range of potential issues impact on the complex lives of many of our EAL learners. Some of the factors are beyond the remit of the school, while others are very much within the school's sphere of influence.

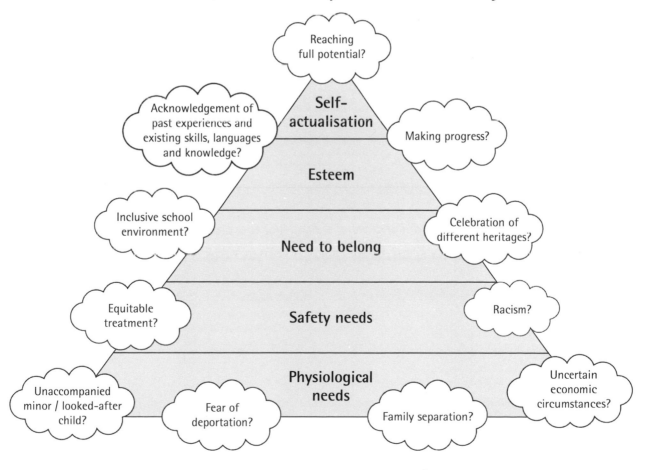

Knowing about the backgrounds, aptitudes and interests of our EAL learners equips us with critical information to plan the most appropriate kinds of provision for them. As may be seen in the chart below, there may be a wide variety of experience in a learner's background.

The background and experience of EAL learners

DfES (2007) Pupil Language Data: 'First Language may be defined as any language other than English that a child was exposed to during early development and continues to be exposed to in the home or community.'

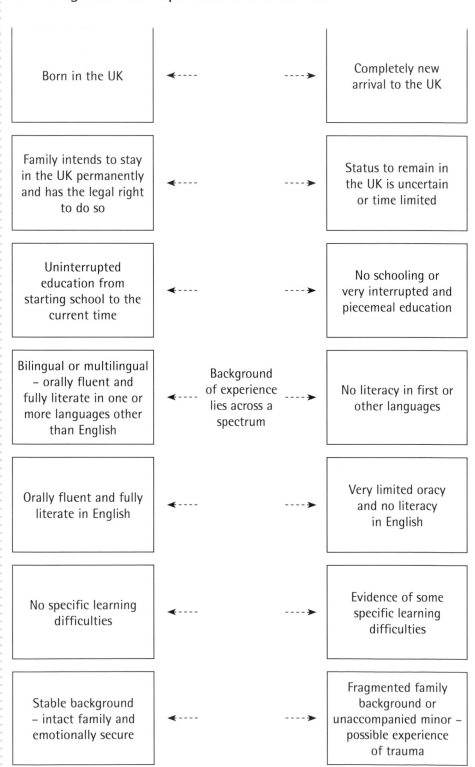

Where do our EAL learners come from and why?

It is always dangerous to make generalisations about patterns and trends because the movement of people around the world changes rapidly. However, the table below lists some fairly common reasons for children and their families being in or coming to the UK in recent years.

Reasons for being in / coming to the UK	Country of origin / languages
First- or second-generation families	Established communities – immigration since the 1950s, particularly from countries/regions in the British Commonwealth (e.g. Caribbean, India, Pakistan, Bangladesh)
To seek asylum – some families may have refugee status or be seeking extended leave to remain through the asylum system	A large number of countries including • Kurdish families from Iraq, Iran, Syria or Turkey • Eritrea, Zimbabwe, Democratic Republic of Congo, Afghanistan, Somalia, Sri Lanka
EU accession – economic migrants	Families mainly from Poland, Slovakia, Lithuania
Government job recruitment • NHS • transport industries • armed forces • hotel and leisure industries	• Tagalog speakers from the Philippines • Polish bus drivers • Chilean families (Navy), Nepali families (Army) • Portuguese
Parents and other family members may be working for universities or studying at university	Especially Arabic speakers from the Middle East, Chinese and Japanese families – but families may come from any country
Gypsy, Roma and Traveller families	In particular Roma from eastern Europe – Romani speakers

Food for thought

Remember that bilingualism is the norm rather than the exception in most countries of the world.

What is bilingualism?

In England the term is currently used to refer to pupils who live in two languages, who have access to, or need to use, two or more languages at home and at school. It does not mean that they have fluency in both languages or that they are competent and literate in both languages.

Hall *et al.* (2001), p. 5.

This working definition of being bilingual includes EAL learners, but encompasses the important notion that all language experience contributes to a learner's educational competence and sense of identity. Bilingual pupils may coexist within a number of linguistic realities, changing between languages as required (known as code-switching).

Learning many languages

Faisal was born in the Sylhet region of Bangladesh but his family moved to the capital, Dhaka, when he was young. He came with his family to the UK in February 2007 and soon after that enrolled at his local junior school in Year 4. He is currently in Year 6. With his parents he speaks Sylheti, a dialect of Bengali, and with his siblings he speaks English. While in Bangladesh he began to learn Bengali, which he now continues to study at a Saturday community language class, and he is on Book 3. He also attends a mosque, where he is learning to recite Arabic from the Qur'an. He understands some Hindi as he is an avid watcher of Bollywood movies at home. At school he is learning French and developing his competence in English.

Bilingual learners potentially have a wide spectrum of language experience – a learner may:

- be fully bilingual (or multilingual) – with fluent oracy and literacy in all their languages

- have partial literacy in several languages including English

- be proficient in English but have low literacy levels in their first language

- be literate in their first language and learning EAL

- have oral skill in their first language, but no literacy in their first language or English – these learners may have had interrupted schooling or may never have been to school.

How does a learner acquire a second language?

Imagine you, as an adult, have just moved to live in a new country or have gone there for an extended holiday. It is more than likely that you will wish to learn some of the local language. Perhaps you already have some ability in this language. Maybe it is a completely new one. As a beginner, you will tend to remain quiet rather than talking, but all the time you will be observing and internalising huge quantities of language, even if you are unaware of this. Depending on circumstances, you may begin to learn language associated with familiar and everyday occurrences such as shopping, finding places or the more obvious vocabulary and simple phrases associated with your work. You will find that colloquial language begins to stick when you are presented with repetitive situations and when you are continually immersed in the language and culture. As time passes, you will become more confident about trying new things and you will soon start to be able to apply language learned in one context to another. Within a fairly short period of time you will have reached a point where you have enough language to suit your immediate purposes. What happens next is dependent on whether you have the determination to start to learn more formal language.

Theories about language learning

There are a number of ideas about how languages are learned. One early theory about bilingualism suggests that the two languages exist together in balance. Pictured as a set of scales, the first language diminishes as a second language is acquired. This suggestion implies there is no interrelationship between the two languages, and it has led to misunderstandings such as that bilingual learners

Food for thought

Research tells us that the younger you are when you start learning a language, the greater the level of proficiency you will acquire. By comparison, in general, the older you are, the faster you will pick it up.

Food for thought

Research tells us that it takes a beginner between five and seven years to develop full academic proficiency in English.

are inferior to monolingual learners and that the brain has the capacity for one language only.

A more accepted theory holds that knowledge of one language supports the development of subsequent languages. This idea may be expressed using the metaphor of icebergs. In this model the tips of icebergs symbolise the surface features of different languages, like vocabulary and grammar, whereas the larger quantity of ice below the water-line represents cognitive and linguistic awareness or a 'common underlying proficiency' (Cummins 1984).

First language   Second language

Common underlying proficiency

BICS – basic interpersonal communicative skills

CALP – cognitive academic language proficiency

Jim Cummins also coined the terms BICS and CALP (Cummins 1979). BICS (basic interpersonal communicative skills) is 'here and now language', everyday communication that tends to be predominately literal in form. CALP is the application of *cognitive* language for conceptual learning, such as analysis, synthesis and evaluation. It is also the use of *academic* language, characterised, for example, by more passive sentence construction, use of vocabulary with Greek and Latin roots and the ability to abstract ideas using simile, metaphor and personification.

In the iceberg model above, two (or more) languages develop alongside each other, and it is very typical for a learner to be more competent in one than in the other. The theory suggests that the common underlying proficiency represents the ability to use cognitive and academic language in a way that is common to all languages. The implication is that once learned, this proficiency can be transferred to the learning of any additional language. Where both languages continue to be developed, there is considerable evidence that this conveys intellectual advantage on the learner. This is a powerful argument for encouraging EAL learners to continue learning their first language alongside English.

Language and learning characteristics of EAL pupils

Beginner EAL

The term 'beginner EAL' is often used to describe pupils who have been learning English for a period of up to two years. While it is true to say that all beginners are at an early stage in terms of their ability to understand and use English, it needs to be remembered that this stage describes a range of abilities. At one end of the scale there are pupils who have recently arrived in the UK speaking little or no English, and at the other there are those who have been attending UK schools for anything up to two years. Pupils who are already in school may be able to communicate quite competently using everyday language – the language they hear at home and in the playground. It can be said that they have acquired, or are in the process of acquiring, their BICS (Cummins 1979). For some pupils BICS will be acquired quite quickly, for others it will take longer. Two years is a rough measure.

It is easy to think of all new arrivals as beginners in English, but this is not the case. Many pupils arrive in school with some understanding of and ability to use English for communication and learning. They include:

- children who have grown up in bilingual families where one parent is a fluent speaker of English

- children from countries where English is used widely (e.g. Nigeria)

- children who have transferred from schools in the UK

- children who have had English language lessons in their home country.

Typical characteristics and behaviour of beginner EAL learners

Listening/ understanding	• Pupils may be silent for a period of time, perhaps up to 6 months, during which time they are looking, listening, absorbing and processing new information • Pupils are likely to show evidence of understanding more than they are able to say
Speaking English	• Pupils are likely to use simple words and short sentences • Talk is likely to focus on things in the immediate environment
Reading English	• Pupils' ability to decode may mask their limited ability to understand what is being read • Pupils will be reliant on pictures, repetitive structures and familiar contexts for understanding
Writing English	• Pupils may have difficulty in forming legible letters if they are more familiar with a non-Roman script • Pupils may experience difficulty with directionality if they have used scripts with right–left or up–down directionality • Pupils are likely to use grammatical structures that reflect the way they talk • Pupils are likely to be slow to finish their written work
National Curriculum levels in other subjects	• Levels are likely to be significantly below those of their monolingual peers in English • Levels may be higher where content is less dependent on ability to communicate in English • Levels may be higher if pupils have received a full education before arriving in the UK
Social relationships	• Pupils may be excited about using their newly acquired English and want to talk to everyone • Pupils may be withdrawn, quiet and anxious, and display low levels of self-esteem • Pupils may display inappropriate behaviour • Pupils are likely to copy the actions and behaviour of others • Pupils may seek out the company of other first language speakers

Beware

If a pupil sounds fluent in English when talking to friends, it doesn't mean they are academically fluent.

Advanced EAL

The term 'advanced EAL learner' is often used to describe pupils who have been learning English for a while, perhaps for two or more years. These pupils are generally confident in their ability to use and manipulate English to express themselves effectively in most social and more abstract academic situations. They are in the process of developing, or have developed, their CALP (Cummins 1979). Research tells us that it takes between three to five years to develop CALP. However, if pupils do not have sufficient exposure to English, the motivation to learn and the support to do so, they may plateau and in some cases never reach full academic proficiency.

Typical characteristics and behaviour of advanced EAL learners

Speaking/ listening	• Everyday language used in place of the required cognitive and academic language of the curriculum • Talk extended to things that are outside the immediate environment • Errors relate more to the use of grammar than to the selection of words
Reading	• Difficulty in understanding age-appropriate curriculum texts
Writing	• More confident than monolingual peers in some aspects e.g. metaphorical and figurative language • Less confident in the adaptation to a variety of genres and correct use of adverbials, modal verbs, prepositions and subject–verb agreement
Speaking, listening, reading, writing	• Some learners can plateau for quite long periods of time in any of the four strands of English without appropriate intervention
National Curriculum levels in other subjects	• Equal to or slightly below those of monolingual peers • Above those of monolingual peers if approaching full fluency in two (or more) languages
Social relationships	• Often more integrated than beginner EAL learners

Language acquisition versus language learning

EAL learners need the opportunity to acquire language naturally within a meaningful context.

You may believe that the best way of supporting your beginner EAL learners is to provide them with specialist language teaching outside the classroom. Research tells us this is not the case. Why is that? To answer this question we need to think about how young children develop understanding of their first language. Would you sit down with your 2-year-old child to explain the grammatical rules governing the use of -s or -es to create the plural forms of nouns? No, of course you wouldn't. So how is it that one day Ellie is able to use these language features perfectly and say to you, 'Ellie washing dishes'? How did it happen? Could it have anything to do with the ninety-nine times that you sang 'The wheels on the bus' or with that wet Monday morning when you were both looking out of the window and counting the buses as they passed by?

Language acquisition occurs most effectively in meaningful contexts that generate a real need and/or desire to use language naturally. For Ellie this was the context of the home. For EAL learners in schools there are two main contexts:

◑ **curriculum context**: generates a need/desire to understand and apply new skills, process and content

◑ **classroom context**: generates a need/desire to understand and interact with both the environment and other pupils.

While focusing on communication in a meaningful context, Ellie picked up or acquired the grammatical rules and vocabulary subconsciously. This is language acquisition and it is quite different from language learning – that is, the conscious teaching and learning of grammatical rules, vocabulary, and so on. It is how we develop the ability to understand and speak fluently.

A theory proposed by Stephen Krashen (1981) is that grammatical features are usually acquired in a natural order similar to, but not the same as, those acquired by first-language speakers. Rules for adding -ing to verbs (playing), adding -s to make plurals (toys) and the use of the verb 'to be' (she is) are acquired early. Adding -s to the end of the third person singular, a rule we consider to be quite simple, is usually acquired late.

It would be reasonable to assume that language teaching could be used to speed up the acquisition process – for example, by teaching the third person singular rule early. However, research suggests that this is not the case. Knowing how a rule works and being able to use it fluently in quick-fire conversation are two entirely different things. The ability to manipulate grammatical rules is not acquired through the repetitive practising of exercises designed to drill the message home, but through understanding information around us within the immediate context.

Conscious grammar learning does not always work for beginner EAL learners, although some pupils educated abroad may have been exposed to this type of teaching. For beginner EAL learners with little or no English, the teaching of grammatical rules, even simple ones, tends to lack meaning. Time for pupils to look and listen is far more supportive at this stage. Conscious grammar learning is most effective when it is used to fill in gaps that advanced EAL learners may have in their acquisition of particular grammatical features. It is most effectively used to support writing because writing provides sufficient time for learners to remember the rules and consider how they might be applied.

Even though it may not appear so at first, the classroom really is the best place for all your EAL learners, except for very specific, time-limited interventions.

Comprehensible input leads to comprehensible output

Although curriculum and classroom contexts generate a real need and desire for pupils to understand and interact, alone they may be insufficient for language acquisition to occur fully. So how can we ensure our EAL learners, once in the classroom, understand age-appropriate curriculum content and acquire the next stage of fluency in English?

Case study

Making input accessible to EAL learners

As part of a course of study, 'Britain since the 1930s', a Year-5 class is working on an evacuation topic. The class teacher has sourced a podcast from the internet about evacuation. While the podcast may be appropriate for many white British monolingual pupils, it may not be immediately accessible to most EAL learners.

A more effective approach might involve any/all of the following.

Context: additional curriculum-setting	Visit to museum (e.g. local sites) or national venues (e.g. Imperial War Museum)
Multimodal approaches that provide additional linguistic content	Holding and looking at artefacts (gas masks, tin hats, ration books, etc.)
	Looking at source material (Pathé, National Archives, TV news / radio broadcasts, photographs, maps and displays)
	Viewing clips from TV/DVD (e.g. documentaries, dramas such as *Goodnight Mister Tom*)
Modified language and gestures / body language	Listening to a short talk using simple sentences with reference to objects in the immediate environment – plenty of mime and gesture
First language	Providing dual language pamphlets and displays, translated audio narrations, websites with translation options, bilingual presenters and interpreters
Prior knowledge of the world	Providing a cultural perspective: refugees around the world

In the above outline, the input is made comprehensible through context and approaches that introduce language, or opportunities for language development, more naturally than via an academic podcast. While consciously focusing on the meaning of what is being said, the EAL learner is exposed to a vast range of grammatical structures and contextualised vocabulary (the longer the input, the greater the exposure). Some language will already have been acquired by the learner, much of it will be beyond them, and some will be just beyond their current competence. With the right scaffolds, it is the elements that are immediately outside their capacity that a learner will begin to acquire. The specific language acquired will be different for each learner and dependent on whether they are a beginner, an advanced EAL learner or somewhere in between.

Learning from a more competent helper

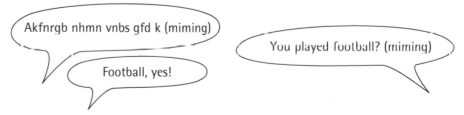

Lev Vygotsky (1896–1934) put forward the theory of the zone of proximal development – that the more you interact with others, the more they interact with you and therefore the more opportunities there are to hear structures a bit beyond your level of competence. When the speaker, whether a peer or adult helper, modifies their speech and uses gestures and other visual resources to help understanding, you have more chance of acquiring new words and grammatical structures. Here are a few points to bear in mind:

- Pupils are generally as good as, if not better than, practitioners at judging how their language needs to be modified so that other pupils can understand them.
- Pupils working with EAL learners need to be competent users of English. This is why it is not a good idea to group EAL learners only with each other.
- Using adults to support EAL learners does not in itself guarantee success; what matters is the quality of the interaction.

As a fundamental principle, practitioners need to plan as many opportunities as possible for pupils to talk and interact with more competent users of English; for example:

- practitioner–pupil interaction during whole-class teaching sessions and guided group work
- pupil–pupil interaction through talk partners and small-group collaborative activities.

Summary

EAL learners are not a homogeneous group. Whether educated abroad or born in the UK, each child comes with particular strengths and weaknesses. Research shows us the importance of:

- building upon prior learning
- maintaining the first language
- facilitating the natural acquisition of language within the mainstream curriculum
- providing intervention to plug specific gaps in learning
- offering comprehensible input in curriculum delivery
- using oracy as a vehicle to develop literacy
- using more competent peers and adults to support language acquisition.

Chapter 2
Effective assessment strategies for all EAL learners

This chapter examines the full range of assessments required in the creation of an early profile for new arrival EAL learners, as well as more ongoing formative and summative assessment for more advanced learners. The interface between EAL and special educational needs (SEN) is covered in detail as well as consideration for those students who might be described as being gifted and/ or talented (G&T). Finally, there is a focus on target-setting, monitoring pupil progress and developing data tracking systems.

Principles of assessment

Assessment is at the heart of teaching and learning. For EAL learners it is essential to view assessment flexibly. This is exemplified by the gathering of different kinds of data in a wide variety of contexts.

Assessment for EAL learners:

○ must recognise prior learning, including proficiency in first language

○ should arise from and inform teaching and learning

○ takes different forms: summative, formative and diagnostic

○ needs to recognise what learners can do rather than what they can't do

○ has to provide ways of assessing beginners that do not rely on the ability to communicate in English

○ needs to be multifaceted, involving a range of assessments in different social contexts – for example, whole class, small groups, pairs, pupil-to-adult and individual

○ should involve all individuals who know the learner well – for example, parents/carers

○ must directly involve learners through a process of dialogue, with practitioners and peers, and via self-assessment.

The appropriateness of traditional testing

As a general rule EAL learners, particularly those relatively new to English, do not fare well in diagnostic and standardised tests such as reading tests, Qualifications and Curriculum Development Agency (QCDA) optional tests and Cognitive Ability Tests (CATs), Standard Assessment Tests (SATs) and the forthcoming single-level tests. This may continue to be the case for a significant time in an EAL learner's educational career. The level of English required for the learner to demonstrate what they know and can do is obviously

Useful resource

NALDIC ITTSEAL (2009) Assessment for learning – working with pupils learning EAL: http://www. naldic.org.uk/ITTSEAL2/ite/ EALAssessmentforlearning.cfm the main barrier. These kinds of test may also present a cultural challenge. For example, CAT tests and those purporting to measure IQ will be unfamiliar to most children educated abroad. Other tests are also likely to pose problems because they will inherently make socio-cultural assumptions of knowledge that may be absent in children who have lived abroad.

Sometimes children are tested soon after they arrive at a school, but delaying testing until they have settled is likely to give a more accurate picture of their abilities. If traditional tests have to be administered, the results should be treated with extreme caution in order to avoid inappropriate teaching and learning provision.

Formative assessment – building an assessment profile

Building an assessment profile is an essential first step in ensuring effective provision for new-arrival EAL learners. The most useful profiles consist of a patchwork of information gleaned from different types of assessment in a range of contexts – for example, conversations with teaching assistants (TAs), notes, annotated samples of work, recorded audio samples, discussions with the pupil and their own self-assessment.

Food for thought

Assessment of an EAL learner's ability in their first language may give an early indication of their wider cognitive ability.

Building a profile can also be useful for other pupils, including black and minority ethnic (BME) pupils or EAL learners born and educated fully in the UK. Assessing pupils in a range of ways and through different tasks will give you a more rounded picture of their achievements so far. This will help you to identify strengths, gaps and the next steps in terms of provision.

An assessment profile should contain:

- ◗ details of previous education and academic achievement (this will be covered in more detail in Chapter 4)

- ◗ assessment of proficiency in the first and other languages

- ◗ assessment of ability to understand and use English across the curriculum – listening, speaking, reading and writing

- ◗ assessment of ability in other subjects

- ◗ observation of classroom interaction in a range of contexts.

Assessment of first and other languages

For EAL learners, particularly new arrivals, it is really useful to establish the full range of languages that they have already experienced. It is common for EAL learners to have proficiency in more than one language, and they will typically have a range of ability within the four strands of speaking, listening, reading and writing. Finding out when and with whom they use these languages may help to create a fuller picture of an EAL learner's linguistic repertoire.

Beware ...
of thinking that it is only worth making a first language assessment if there is an interpreter/translator available.

Beware
Features of speaking, reading and writing that exist in English may not exist in other languages. Some languages have no written form – for example, Sylheti, which is usually defined as a dialect of Bengali.

First language assessment

When it comes to a pupil's first language, it is really critical to try to establish their proficiency in speaking, listening, reading and writing; and in particular whether they are working below, at or above an age-appropriate level. In conjunction with other details, such as when the learner started school and how long they have studied the specific language, obtaining information about their proficiency will alert you to any potential problems and to whether they might be considered to be gifted or talented.

Don't be put off by the thought that it might be problematic to get interpreters and translators involved. A lot of information can be gleaned from just listening to pupils talking and reading and by scrutinising a sample of their writing. Of course, having an interpreter report how a child interacts through talk and how they respond to a reading task, and obtaining a translation of a writing sample will be more beneficial.

Speaking and listening

Providing an opportunity for learners to talk in their first language throughout the school day is generally good practice, whether with peers, pupils in different age groups or adults. There will be opportunities to observe this happening naturally, or it may be possible to facilitate a more formal session, perhaps embedded within curriculum context. A bilingual practitioner could facilitate such a session and provide useful feedback about the interaction that may be vital in identifying a specific learning difficulty or confirming there is no such problem.

Reading

Hearing an EAL learner read an appropriate text in their first language can be very revealing. It is important to choose a text that meets the age and ability of the child. This could be done by presenting them with a range of texts set at different levels. Care needs to be taken not to demean a learner by, for example, presenting them with a text that is much too easy or hard for them. A reading assessment, where possible, should include reading part or all of a text as well as an opportunity to delve into the story to check for understanding. In an ideal world this would involve a bilingual practitioner, but a lot can be gleaned from just listening to a child read in their first language, even if you don't understand it yourself. Look out for the following, for example:

- general fluency

- pace

- intonation and expression – where relevant

- self-correction

- using strategies to decode unfamiliar words.

Of course, having an interpreter present will enable a fuller assessment of the reading capability of the learner. They should be able to check whether the learner is reading for meaning as well as whether their reading ability is age appropriate.

Writing

A writing sample in the first language can be tremendously informative, whether a translation can ultimately be obtained or not. Embedding the writing task in a familiar context will assist the learner in demonstrating their true writing ability. For example, pupils will be more likely to be able to write at length about familiar situations such as their family, life in their home country or a hobby. Writing about a book they have read in their first language is also a good springboard for generating a useful sample of writing.

The writing sample above was obtained from a Year-4 Nepali speaker after she had read a KS2 text entitled 'The Hare and the Tortoise'. Even as a non-Nepali writer it is possible to see the following features:

○ a reasonable quality of handwriting

○ writing at some length

○ absence of capitalisation (capitalisation does not exist in Nepali)

○ punctuation – commas and full stops (| is a full stop in Nepali)

○ self-correction

○ a lack of paragraphing – although the sample is relatively brief

○ repetitive use of certain connectives (e.g. 'and' is र in Nepali).

Familiarity with different scripts will give you confidence in looking for this kind of evidence. Knowing, for example, that Nepali does not have capitalisation will allow the absence of this feature in the writing sample to be disregarded.

If a Nepali translator is available, they will be able to provide a more sophisticated insight into the sample of writing. In this case a bilingual practitioner was able to report that, because the pupil had attended an English medium school in Nepal, the sample of writing was age appropriate.

Knowing that a learner can write at a comparable level to peers of a similar age (and background) should indicate that they have academic potential that may be described as average or better – certainly for literacy, anyway.

Curriculum-related assessment

For learners within the Early Years Foundation Stage (EYFS) it is particularly important that any assessment is made within the context of play-based provision, either through adult-led or child-initiated learning activities. Generally, assessment for older EAL learners should occur in both formal and informal situations, across the curriculum and in a range of social situations. Some ideas for initial assessment are shown below.

Context	Potential observations / assessment opportunities
Listening	Listening attentively and following instructions Reaction to non-verbal cues
Speaking	Asking for help Contribution to oral discussion – whole class, groups, pairs, with adults
Reading	Familiarity with books – fiction and non-fiction Ability to decode Use of contextual clues – visuals Using different strategies to identify unfamiliar words Reading for meaning
Writing	Handwriting and writing directionality, drawing/painting Ability to copy Note-taking and annotating More formal writing
Practical	Motor skills and coordination ICT – keyboard and mouse skills Map skills – knowledge of directionality, distance, grid references, symbols Music – awareness of pitch, tempo, rhythm
Mathematics	Knowledge of number, symbols, tables Use of calculator Awareness and experience of range of UK mathematics topics
Social	Interaction with peers – formal and informal situations

Targets for EAL learners

Targets for EAL learners, as with all pupils, need to be SMART – specific, measurable, achievable, realistic and time limited. This means they should be:

- *specific* – expressed as a single entity and with a degree of security – for example, 'sometimes', 'usually', 'with support'

- *measurable* – linked to the QCA/NASSEA (Northern Association of Support Services for Equality and Achievement) EAL scale or to the lower levels of the National Curriculum

○ *achievable* – developmentally just within reach of the learner, with scaffolded support

○ *realistic* – set within real learning contexts

○ *time limited* – short term, demonstrable within a single activity or long term, within a unit of work.

Some examples of SMART short-term language targets

	Speaking/Listening	Reading	Writing
Beginner EAL	Follow one-step instructions given to the class Talk about immediate experiences	Understand the direction of English print Read labels around the school	Copy single words and names Write a subject–verb–object sentence with support every lesson
Advanced EAL	Use metaphorical expressions Secure use of register in a specific context	Use intonation to convey meaning Identify specific genre of a text	Secure use of past, present and future tenses Use direct speech in writing

Individual language plans

EAL learners will also benefit from individual language plans (ILPs). These are detailed language specifications for speaking, listening, reading and writing aimed at the specific developmental stage of the EAL learner. Below is an example of an ILP developed for a new-arrival beginner EAL learner.

Individual language plan – speaking and listening

Name:		Class teacher:		Year group:

Start date:			
Targets	Targets	Targets	Targets
Greetings Hello, how are you? I'm fine, thanks. Good morning Goodbye	**Identifying themselves and others** My name is ... What's your name? How old are you? I am ... I am a boy/girl. I speak ...	**Extend vocabulary** Names of animals, food/drink, vehicles, household objects, clothes, toys (use visuals) Singular and plural forms of nouns	**Parts of the body** Games: Simon Says, Beetle Drive (parts of the human body are collected by throwing a dice) Song: 'Heads, shoulders, knees and toes'
Classroom language Names of basic items in the classroom can be practised by using such prompts as: Give me a/the ... Show me the ... What's this? It's a ... What are these? Introduce possessive pronouns my/your/his/her	**Social language** Please, thank you, no thanks, sorry, excuse me. May I go to the toilet, please? May I go out to play? May I have a book/pencil/pen/ruler? etc. Instructions: close/open your book, put your pen/pencil down, sit down, stand up, put your hand up, etc. Game: Simon Says	**Adjectives** big – small good – bad happy – sad fast – slow new – old open – shut hot/warm – cold thin – fat same – different first – last (select opposites as appropriate for the age and ability of the pupil)	**Clothes** What's he/she wearing? He/she is wearing ... What are you wearing? I'm wearing ...

Colours	Ask/answer questions about number, learn basic vocabulary	Days of the week	Verb tenses
What colour is it? It's ... (colour name). Introduce prepositions with classroom items already learnt: e.g. in, on, under. Where's the ...? It's in/on/under the ...	Learn numbers up to 10, 20, 50, 100 and over as appropriate. How many? How many ... are there? There are ... Operation signs and words: add, take away, multiply, divide	What day is it today? It's ... What day was it yesterday? It was ... What day is it tomorrow?	Present continuous: What are you doing? I am ... -ing. What is he/she doing? He/she is ... -ing. Game: Charades Simple past: introduce with time words: e.g. yesterday, last week
Date achieved: Comments:	Date achieved: Comments:	Date achieved: Comments:	Date achieved: Comments:

Adapted with permission from Portsmouth Ethnic Minority Achievement Service (2008).

Summative assessment
Assessment of English

The achievement profiles of EAL learners are likely to be more uneven than those of other pupils. Practitioners will need to use a range of evidence and assessment frameworks to ensure that these learners have the maximum opportunity to demonstrate their progress.

Some EAL learners, particularly those newly arrived, have quite limited proficiency in English and it may be difficult to assess specific levels because they fall off the bottom of the English National Curriculum scale.

Find out more:

A language in common: assessing English as an additional language: http://www.qcda.gov.uk/5739.aspx

In 'A language in common' the Qualifications and Curriculum Authority (QCA 2000) provides a nationally recognised scale for assessing EAL learners who are working at pre-National Curriculum level 2 in English. It gives a set of four step descriptors for speaking, listening, reading and writing that enables a secure baseline assessment from which to measure small but significant progress in the four skills.

The language in common steps can be helpful in showing very early progress in learning English, but many specialist teachers feel they are not extensive enough. Some schools and teachers use different ways to chart a learner's progress in using English in a school setting. These alternative scales may:

❍ be adapted for different age groups

❍ look at the use of English across the curriculum

❍ show the journey from the very earliest stages of learning English to being fully fluent.

Whatever scales, steps or levels are used, be aware of the following:

❍ Some learners will move through the scales quite rapidly; others will not.

❍ It is typical for EAL learners to be working at different levels in speaking, listening, reading and writing.

P scales: differentiated performance criteria that outline assessment for pupils working below level 1 of the National Curriculum.

Find out more:

DCSF (2009) Assessing pupils' progress (APP): http://nationalstrategies. standards.dcsf.gov.uk/ primary/assessment/ assessingpupilsprogressapp

○ Learners may show quite different profiles from one subject to the next.

Use of the P scales is not appropriate unless the EAL learner has a designated SEN. Many schools are now implementing Assessing Pupils' Progress (APP) to provide a detailed way of assessing progress in learning English and other subjects and developing targets for the next bit of learning. In order to use AfL and APP effectively with bilingual learners, training should be geared towards teachers having the appropriate subject and pedagogic knowledge so that they can assess language development as well as curricular learning. Teachers of all bilingual children need to be aware of the aspects of children's language development, as well as of their learning needs in particular subject areas, when making a judgement about performance and achievement. Many of these aspects of language are linked to:

○ AF 5: Vary sentences for clarity, purpose and effect

○ AF 6: Write with technical accuracy of syntax and punctuation in phrases, clauses and sentences

○ AF 7: Select appropriate and effective vocabulary.

They include accurate and appropriate use of determiners, prepositions, verb tenses, modals and subject–verb agreements. While these may not affect judgements about National Curriculum levels at levels 1 and 2, they are crucial if children are to achieve level 4 and beyond as many of them in turn affect progress in the other assessment focuses. Information from assessments of children learning EAL need to inform language development targets as well as ensuring progression in the core subject areas.

For assessing reading, evidence should be gathered from across the curriculum, using a range of strategies through which children can demonstrate comprehension.

Sample of Year-6 writing – unaided, but with significant teaching preparation

The sample of writing on the opposite page is by a relatively recent entrant (12 months ago) to the UK. The pupil clearly demonstrates the use of a flashback in the opening of the story. He has demonstrated that, within the timescale, he is writing simple sentences with connectives. There is evidence that he is starting to grasp some irregular verbs in the past tense. The target this pupil has been set has been to continue to work on the past tense, concentrating on determiners, and to focus on organising writing in paragraphs. This pupil is currently working at a secure level 2. It should be remembered that this piece of work represents a snapshot in time and needs to be considered alongside a range of other written evidence.

Introduction

evidence of a flashback — I am siting in library and reading a book about under water boats. Then I remembered that what hapened 5 year ago. I was sleeping in my bed on under water boat. Then I heared a big bang and alarm. I woke up and man up to a captin. He said that we hit an iceberg. I ran to the rest of sailors. I help them to ged out from an iceberg. I asked them are you all right? They said not really. I felt Ffmezing and fritened. Hearving bit of But I still can see someone in here.

use of question marks

I asked "Who is in here? it is was a woman. Who are you. I asked I am a women witch wanted to ged to your boat. I helped her f og ed out.

speech marks needed here to denote speech — We sank and meand captin were resoved. I'm a lifeboat. We become to be friends. We was proud of us. I didind know how to ged out from boat... I can smell water. I can hear alarm. I was thincking about my family. I didind know how to ged out from the boat. The way out cant open but i found 22 under water swimming cosivms. I told that to

irregular verbs here

can/could captin. He says he is called for help. Then I felt in say/said trouble. I Qvickly went to wear one. I went out from my boat. I saw rescue boat straight in front of me.

use of exclamation marks needed — I told them to help me rescue them. And then they said "We can help you." I said "ok". We were rescued.

Wow! Agnes your writing is really improving (2HP)

can = present tense
could = past tense

Pupil working at a level 2. (secure)

Developmental English language features of EAL learners

As has been described previously, in most cases knowledge and skills in one language can support the development of another, such as English. However, it is also the case that certain surface features of one language can transfer across during the early stages of acquiring a second.

Sometimes it is possible to guess the nationality of an EAL learner by listening to them talking. Perhaps the accent, inappropriate use of plurals, odd use of tense, a clumsy word order or some other feature has transferred over because the learner is applying the correct use of their first language to English.

A useful summary for some languages may be found here: http://www3.hants.gov.uk/education/ema/ema-resource/ema-lcr

These kinds of feature in oral language will also be evident in writing. Practitioners will benefit from knowing the typical EAL writing features related to the language concerned as this will help identify whether recurring errors are developmental rather than caused by a lack of understanding.

More about writing

Research by Lynne Cameron and Sharon Besser in 2004 into the writing of advanced EAL learners at KS2 was based upon scrutiny of SATs scripts from pupils achieving levels 3, 4 and 5. Their aim was to identify the distinctive features of writing by advanced learners of EAL. The report highlighted particular strengths in writing, such as the highly metaphorical and figurative writing of many EAL learners. However, the study also pinpointed specific difficulties such as less 'confident adaptation to a variety of genres' and incorrect use of adverbials, modal verbs, prepositions and subject–verb agreement.

The details of the report inform best practice in assessing pupils' progress and will focus practitioners' attention on planning to meet specific weaknesses in writing for advanced learners.

The full report may be downloaded here: http://www.dcsf.gov.uk/research/data/uploadfiles/RR586.pdf

Assessment of mathematical ability

As a general rule, EAL learners should progress at a similar rate in their mathematical learning to their peers, unless there is some specific learning difficulty such as dyscalculia. A secure baseline assessment is the first step to ensuring effective teaching and learning.

Here are a few points for consideration:

- EAL learners, particularly those new to English, may find it more difficult than others to demonstrate their true ability in standard tests.

- Enabling EAL learners to think, talk and write in their stronger first language, where appropriate, will enable them to access the curriculum more effectively and is likely to lead to a more accurate assessment of their true ability. Use of bilingual practitioners and same first-language peer-talk partners (see Chapter 3) will assist the assessment process.

- For new arrivals, there are likely to be gaps or differences in a pupil's knowledge or skills due to the fact that there are areas which aren't covered or are covered at a later age by the curriculum in their home country.

$$ax^2 + bx + c = 0$$

- EAL learners may have knowledge and skills in some topics that are way beyond that of their peers – for example, algebra, trigonometry and certain numerical operations like long division. This may be due to different curriculum emphasis and possibly a more mechanistic, repetitive style of learning in their home country.

- The conventions of assessment may be unfamiliar to some EAL learners who have been educated abroad – such as the need to demonstrate how a problem is solved, and the idea that there may be many ways to solve the same problem.

- Some aspects of mathematics may contain more demanding language – for example, word problems.

Useful resource

DfES (2003) Assessment in mathematics: toolkit to support pupils for whom English is an additional language: http://nationalstrategies.standards.dcsf.gov.uk/node/151719

Where APP relates to mathematics, beginner EAL learners who are proficient in their first language may benefit from demonstrating and explaining their work through that language, both orally as well as in written form.

Additional needs and EAL
Special Educational Needs and EAL

Historically, there has been some confusion about the distinction between SEN and EAL, and this has often shown itself by too many EAL learners being 'diagnosed' as having SEN. Where a misdiagnosis happens, it inevitably results in inappropriate provision that serves to hinder rather than help the progress of EAL learners.

While it is recognised that for a significant part of their educational careers many EAL learners have some quite specific additional educational needs (AEN), this should not be confused with SEN. For most EAL learners the additional needs are more than likely related to language and socio-cultural factors rather than to medical or cognitive issues. The evidence for this is clear. There appears to be no more likelihood of an EAL learner having SEN than a monolingual pupil.

Here are some examples of misdiagnosis that can lead to inappropriate labelling and consequent poor practice:

> Anwar seems very withdrawn and will not talk to his peers – there must be some specific learning difficulty here.

> Yes, Anwar will be better off in a lower-ability group as the work will be more at his level.

> Dorota needs to be in a lower-ability group as we can then target TA support for her.

> We could also withdraw her from the classroom for 1:1 intervention with a TA.

> Meifeng just can't improve her pronunciation and she doesn't seem to be able to improve even when I speak really slowly.

> Yes, Meifeng continues to make the same mistakes with tense, plurals and correct use of gender. She just doesn't get it – perhaps we need to look for some form of cognitive delay.

Situations like these happen all the time, yet it is more than likely that none of the learners has any specific learning difficulty. The suggested course of actions may serve to hinder their progress, rather than help. It is self-evident, however, that some EAL learners do have SEN. It is sometimes extremely difficult to determine whether an observed phenomenon is SEN related or a typical EAL feature linked to the acquisition of a new language or due to some other socio-cultural factor.

Some questions to ask:

○ Has the school gained a full picture of the child's previous educational experience?

○ Has a full assessment of the first language been conducted, including consideration of whether the learner is working at an age-appropriate level?

○ Does the judgement look beyond raw scores in standard national assessments and tests?

○ Have observations of the pupil been made in a variety of contexts on more than one occasion?

○ Is appropriate classroom provision in place?

○ Do errors in work reflect spoken language, and are they typical of those identified by Cameron and Besser (2004) in their research into advanced EAL learners?

Some practitioners use a diagnostic tool created by Susan Shaw and adapted by Portsmouth EMAS. This consists of a set of filter questions that help tease out the distinction between factors associated with being an EAL learner and those indicators that are more likely to be connected with having SEN: http://www. school-portal.co.uk/GroupDownloadFile.asp?GroupID=710539&ResourceId= 2181454

G&T learners from BME backgrounds

At the other end of the spectrum lies the complex issue of identification and provision for BME learners with a specific gift or talent. EAL learners, in particular, pose an additional challenge because lack of full proficiency in English may mask their true abilities and talents. An inclusive strategy would suggest that the percentage of BME and EAL learners identified in this category would be representative of the overall population, yet evidence shows this is not always the case. Since schools are free to determine the size of their G&T population, it is worth considering whether schools have a flexible approach to identification. In addition, it is important to monitor whether EAL learners who have been identified as G&T are being sufficiently challenged.

Some questions to ask:

○ Is the number of minority ethnic and EAL learners on the G&T register representative of the school population as a whole?

○ Does the school take a flexible approach to identification – that is, looking at academic potential rather than current attainment and recognising talents such as ability in the first language?

○ Do initial assessments for new arrivals capture the essential information to enable early identification of G&T status?

○ Are staff aware of how to adapt teaching and learning to ensure advanced EAL learners have the maximum opportunity to develop their full academic potential?

○ Has the school conducted a self-evaluation using G&T quality standards?

Some useful resources

Module 16 of the REAL project – Supporting gifted and talented learners with English as an additional language: http://nationalstrategies. standards.dcsf.gov.uk/ node/162839

National quality standards in gifted and talented education: http://www.standards.dfes. gov.uk/giftedandtalented/ strategyandstrands/strategy/ Qualstan/

Food for thought
Many EAL learners underattain for significant parts of their educational career as they are still acquiring academic fluency in English. This is perfectly normal, but they will catch up, and in many cases exceed their peers, given time.

Beware ...
of having lower expectations of EAL learners compared to their monolingual peers. For significant parts of their educational career, EAL learners will make more rapid progress, assuming they are exposed to good quality-first teaching and appropriate intervention.

More information may be obtained from the EMA section of the Department for Children, Schools and Families (DCSF) standards site: http://www.standards.dfes.gov.uk/ethnicminorities/

Tracking progress
Some definitions
To begin with, it seems important to define some key terms. For clarity, we should make the distinction between **achievement** and **attainment**.

Achievement – the progress that an individual makes over the course of time. Progress is formative although it is measured by comparing robust data between two specific points.

Attainment – summative, and merely a measure of performance at a moment in time, perhaps on completion of a unit of work, at the end of the year or the end of the key stage. Attainment may be measured via teacher assessment as well as through nationally recognised benchmarks such as QCDA optional tests and SATs.

Comparing attainment between different minority ethnic groups
Both national and local data show that certain groups do perform better than others in national benchmark tests. The reasons for this are varied and complex. Comparisons between the attainment of different ethnic groups should be:

- considered first at school level
- reflective of the local authority context
- set within the national context.

The attainment of different ethnic groups will vary between schools and frequently differ from the overall picture at local authority level. Also, some local authorities / county councils buck the national trend. However, care needs to be taken about comparing the achievement of different groups because the numbers of individuals may be so small that the data can be easily skewed. For example, one Somali pupil in the school may represent a 100 per cent pass/fail rate for the ethnic group Black African.

There are a number of EMA grant-funded projects currently running that have been specifically designed to narrow the attainment gap between certain ethnic groups. Early signs are that the gap is narrowing slowly, but this is no time to be complacent.

The gender issue
Where there are significant numbers of individuals involved, it may make sense to analyse whether there is a gender issue within a particular minority ethnic group. This kind of monitoring can be useful in highlighting particular issues for specific communities – for example, aspirations of parents.

Expected rates of progress for EAL learners
In the example shown on p. 30, two pupils have received their end of KS2 assessment scores. One, a British born monolingual pupil, has reached the

nationally recognised benchmark of 2b. The other, an EAL learner who has been in the country for approximately nine months, has reached level 1c, a very acceptable achievement as the pupil came with very little English oracy and is still developing literacy in their first language.

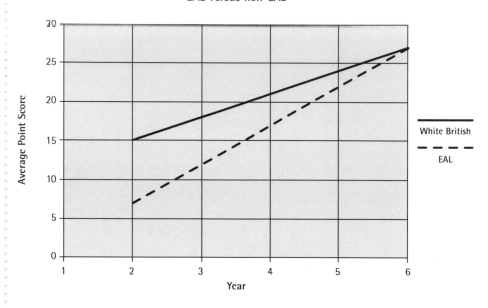

Anticipated rates of progress from Year 2 to Year 6
EAL versus non-EAL

Given nationally recognised rates of progress of about two sub-levels a year, a non-EAL learner would be expected to reach at least the standard attainment of 4b at the end of Year 6. However, given similar rates of achievement for an EAL learner, they would not reach the desired standard. For this reason the trajectory for EAL learners needs to be steeper than normal in order to enable them to catch up with their peers. The kind of aspirational target set for the EAL learner in this scenario is highly achievable, but it will require good quality-first teaching and the implementation of a range of interventions to ensure the targets are met.

Using different data analysis tools

There is a range of different tools available to help schools monitor the progress of their pupils, individually as well as by cohort, within and between key stages, and by comparing the attainment of learners in different circumstances. Such tools support the development of targets at the level of the individual as well as cohort and end-of-key-stage targets. They include Fischer Family Trust data and RAISEonline.

Tracking documents

Tracking pupil progress is an essential link in the assessment chain and, where possible, any information required should be integrated with existing school systems. However, the system should be flexible enough to include extraneous data pertinent to ethnic minority / EAL achievement.

Fischer Family Trust provides data analyses for schools and local authorities to aid self-evaluation and target setting. RAISEonline is a web-based system containing such information as schools' characteristics, pupil attainment and progress data.

This example, a partial tracking document, details the range of additional fields that are particularly important in developing an effective data tracking system for EAL learners.

School's year-by-year data tracking systems

-------------------------------->

Name	Year group	Gender	Date of entry to UK	Country of origin	Ethnicity	First language	EAL?	Literacy in L1?	

Here are a few comments on tracking systems:

○ Tracking systems should include all BME pupils, not just those reported as learning EAL.

○ Date of entry into the UK is a critical piece of information as this may explain underattainment for the early part of a learner's educational career – it will not, however, explain underachievement.

○ Country of origin, ethnicity and first language each add useful information and, more importantly, they add extra fields upon which to analyse data.

○ EAL – bear in mind that not all ethnic minority pupils have an influencing language in their background. Those who do not would not be described as learning EAL. It is a worthwhile field, however, because it can be useful to analyse data in different ways – for example, ethnic minority and/or EAL compared with white British. The number of beginner EAL learners in the school is also required information for the school self-evaluation form.

○ Literacy in first language can be difficult to determine. It is suggested that 'yes' is entered in this field if the learner is working at an age-appropriate level in reading and writing, 'partial' if they have some literacy, and 'none' if they have little or no ability in reading and writing their first language.

○ The specific system used to develop the tracking system needs to be flexible enough to record step descriptors from the QCA EAL scale.

Chapter 3
Catering for language and learning needs of EAL learners

The main focus of this chapter relates to mainstream provision that is common to all EAL learners, advanced as well as beginners. While much of the advice and guidance is about quality-first teaching, this chapter aims to exemplify ways in which good teaching can be modified and/or built upon to meet the distinctive needs of all EAL learners. A key message is that EAL is not just about learning from the perspective of the child; it is also something that needs to be explicitly planned and taught.

Strengths and challenges

The influence of another language in a pupil's background, as well as their own individual cultural experience, presents a quadruple challenge for an EAL learner as they begin to acquire knowledge and skills through the school curriculum. The four elements are these:

- ❍ language development – oracy and literacy in English (and other significant languages in a learner's background)

- ❍ cognitive development – the faculty for processing information

- ❍ academic development – formal application of language across the curriculum

- ❍ adjustment to a culturally bound curriculum – 'Eurocentric' content and unfamiliar teaching approaches.

Different teaching styles and methods – thinking outside the box – learner voice

Cognitive development
- investigating
- exploring
- solving
- analysing
- classifying
- predicting
- hypothesising
- evaluating
- extrapolating

EAL learner

Academic development all subjects
- ideas and concepts
- academic language – e.g. genre and register, vocabulary, figurative language, nominalisations

Language development
English + other languages
- speaking
- listening
- reading
- writing

socio-cultural factors – Eurocentric curriculum – cultural bias or tokenism

Adapted from Thomas and Collier (1997).

EAL pupils generally bring skills and experiences to their learning that add long-term educational benefit. It is well understood that being bilingual is cognitively beneficial and that learners can transfer knowledge about the application of language from their first language across to their learning of English. In general, EAL pupils have a positive attitude to schooling and their families are usually very supportive of the educational process.

Beware ...

of thinking that all EAL learners have the same needs.

The implications for practitioners are wide and varied. While EAL learners have additional hurdles to overcome in their learning, many have the distinct advantage of knowledge and understanding of other languages, which should allow them to catch up with their peers when presented with an inclusive and personalised education.

Basic principles

There are many factors that will affect the achievement and attainment of an EAL learner, as would be the case for any monolingual child. However, the school's treatment of EAL learners and general classroom practice will have the most impact, whether positive or negative. Consider the range of factors affecting the two Year-4 pupils in the following scenarios.

Case study 1 – Dimitri

Dimitri and his family came to the UK in June 2008, and he joined his current school in the middle of Year 3. When he first arrived he was at the early stages of learning English. Conversation with his parents suggested that he was of average ability, although quite good at science. This seemed to be confirmed by ongoing teacher assessment, which also concluded that he was gifted in languages. It was established that he should continue to study Russian at home. Dimitri's class teacher allocated him a class buddy and placed him in a higher-ability group for literacy. He made good progress at school in the first year, and he was assessed as being at level 2a for speaking and listening and at level 2c for reading and writing. His teacher says that he has integrated well into the class.

Case study 2 – Leila

Leila and her family came from Algeria to the UK in July 2008 to seek political asylum. She started school in September 2008 in a Year-3 class. The school established that Leila could speak Arabic and French but was unable to find out much other information because her parents spoke only limited English and a bilingual adult was unavailable at the time to help gather this kind of information. Her parents suggested that Leila should speak only English at home with themselves and her siblings, in order to help her to improve her English. The class teacher decided to allocate Leila to a lower-ability group where she would get focused support from a TA. For the first three months during literacy and languages she was withdrawn for one-to-one intervention sessions. During the first year at the school Leila would rarely speak in class and made slow progress, moving only on to the very lowest levels of the English National Curriculum. Leila seemed to struggle in most subjects, particularly with any reading and writing tasks. She had, however, made good progress in mathematics. The class teacher was concerned that Leila seemed rather withdrawn from the rest of the class.

The differential progress made by the two EAL learners could be explained by a number of different factors. Previous educational experience may have been very different for each child. There may be a significant difference in cognitive ability between the two pupils; for one of them there may even be an SEN issue.

One pupil may be receiving more help and support at home from the family. Perhaps there are cultural, religious or even gender issues at work. It is possible that bullying or racism is a factor. These potential explanations will all need to be considered if an EAL learner makes less progress than expected in their learning. However, these factors are probably not the first place to start looking for explanations. Initially it might be worth considering whether school policy and/or classroom practice needs rethinking.

Here are some core principles regarding provision for EAL learners at whatever stage they are in their acquisition of English. All EAL learners need:

- a safe, welcoming environment, including protection from bullying/racism

- full access to a broad and balanced curriculum

- teaching that builds upon prior learning

- mainstream teaching rather than withdrawal intervention, except in specific cases

- teaching that matches their cognitive ability rather than their level of English

- teaching and learning strategies that scaffold the pupil's understanding of, and ability to use, curriculum-related language

- collaborative approaches where talk is central to learning

- opportunity to utilise ability in first language to support learning of and through English

- maximum opportunities within the curriculum to incorporate the past experiences, knowledge and interests of children from all ethnic backgrounds.

Beware ...
the idea that EAL learners need a 'special' curriculum to cater for their needs.

Understanding the demands of the curriculum
The cognitive challenge
Every activity within a lesson places a range of cognitive challenges before any learner. When planning for EAL learners, like all pupils, it is important to match the cognitive challenge to the ability of the child. We are doing no favours for a pupil if the level of the work is either too simple or too demanding for them. It is important to understand that EAL learners face a double-whammy because not only do they need to tackle the cognitive challenge within any activity, but they also have to overcome the linguistic demands because they are accessing content in a language in which they are not fully proficient for their age. We know that some white British monolingual pupils face this challenge also.

The contextual challenge
Every teacher knows that learning proceeds more rapidly when there is a clear context for learning; when learning objectives are explicit; when there is a natural progression from one activity to the next; and when concepts, even the most abstract, are related to real-world experience. Context is critical, yet sometimes provision for EAL learners ignores this important notion. In worst-

case scenarios EAL learners, particularly those new to English, are withdrawn from class to learn basic English or phonics in a very de-contextualised way, or presented with very academic, linguistically challenging and highly abstract tasks that mean nothing to them.

Meeting the needs of EAL learners is all about finding the right balance of cognitive and linguistic challenge and creating an appropriate context for learning. This balance will obviously be different for every learner.

The Cummins framework

One way of thinking about the relationship between cognitive challenge and context is via the Cummins Framework (Cummins 1984). How can the Cummins Framework inform teaching and learning for EAL learners? Each quadrant describes the level of academic and cognitive challenge and how much context there is to help understanding. Practitioners may use the quadrants to predict the types of strategy required to support EAL learners in any activity or series of activities. It should be understood that no EAL learner fits neatly into any specific quadrant, nor is any particular quadrant just about speaking, reading or writing.

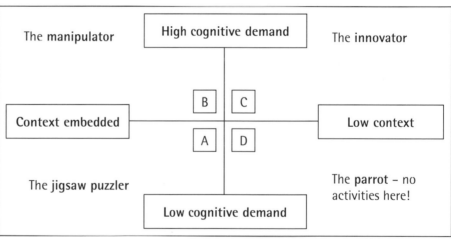

Cognitive academic language proficiency (CALP)

The manipulator | High cognitive demand | The innovator

| B | C |

Context embedded | | Low context

| A | D |

The jigsaw puzzler | Low cognitive demand | The parrot – no activities here!

Basic interpersonal communication skills (BICS)

The terms 'parrot', 'jigsaw puzzler', 'manipulator' and 'innovator' are attributed to Tameside EMAT.

Explaining the quadrants

Quadrant A – characterised by learning scenarios that have a reduced cognitive challenge but an obvious context. Here the focus, within any curriculum area, is on learning by doing. Use of language tends to be more oral and based around the immediacy of the task at hand. Examples include talking about the properties of magnets, sequencing a visual storyboard and identifying vocabulary on a theme in a wordsearch. For learners new to English, particularly those with interrupted or piecemeal educational experience, the lower cognitive challenge can sometimes be counterbalanced by

the elevated linguistic challenge of accessing the demands of the curriculum in a new language.

Quadrant B – a desirable starting point for many EAL learners because activities have a higher cognitive challenge yet still possess a genuine context for learning. Examples here include summarising a set of ideas, talking about the results in an experiment and planning follow-up tests, and rewriting the ending to a familiar traditional tale. Beginner EAL learners will need specific scaffolding to move here from Quadrant A. Similarly, more advanced learners can be shifted into Quadrant C with the appropriate range of support strategies.

Quadrant C – here, activities tend to be more formal and academic. There is a high cognitive challenge but less obvious context. Examples include a philosophical discussion, extracting information from an academic podcast, identifying themes in poetry and writing an imaginary diary extract from the perspective of a historical character. Many EAL learners will need a range of scaffolds to function fully within this quadrant.

Quadrant D – here, activities tend to be weak on learning outcomes as there is little cognitive challenge. Activities include colouring, parroting speech and copying writing. In most cases these kinds of activities should be avoided, even for learners completely new to English.

An example from science – experimenting with paper helicopters

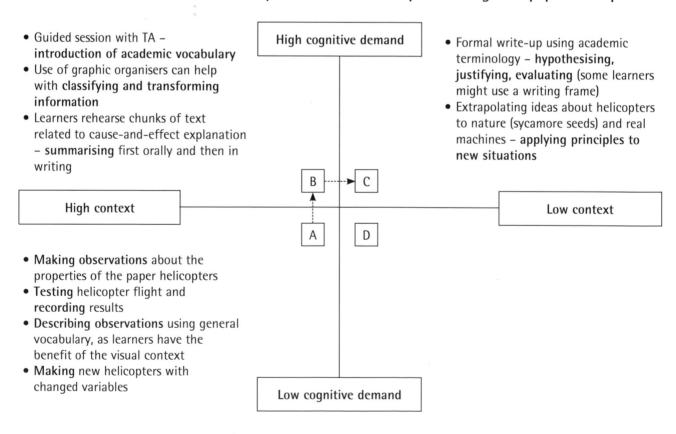

- Guided session with TA – **introduction of academic vocabulary**
- Use of graphic organisers can help with **classifying and transforming information**
- Learners rehearse chunks of text related to cause-and-effect explanation – **summarising** first orally and then in writing

High context

High cognitive demand

Low cognitive demand

Low context

- Formal write-up using academic terminology – **hypothesising, justifying, evaluating** (some learners might use a writing frame)
- Extrapolating ideas about helicopters to nature (sycamore seeds) and real machines – **applying principles to new situations**

- **Making observations** about the properties of the paper helicopters
- **Testing** helicopter flight and **recording** results
- **Describing observations** using general vocabulary, as learners have the benefit of the visual context
- **Making** new helicopters with changed variables

Quadrant A – a TA and a mixed group of Year-4 and Year-5 pupils, including one beginner and one advanced EAL learner, are investigating the flying capability of a range of different paper helicopters. A snapshot of the discussion about the characteristics of one of the paper helicopters is shown below. It illustrates the colloquial nature of unguided 'process talk' (BICS), where pupils tend to avoid using academic language because meaning is made explicit by the visual nature of the activity.

Pupil A – Advanced EAL learner
Pupil B – Beginner EAL learner
Pupil C – White British monolingual learner

Pupil C: This one's a bit taller but …
Pupil A: Thinner.
Pupil C: Yeah, thinner.
Pupil A: It'll stay in air longer time … it's got bigger wings *[indicating the propellers]*.
Pupil B: It heavy … more heavy *[pointing at two paperclips]*.
Pupil C: Yeah … other one only has one.
Pupil A: Might fall quick then.

Quadrant B – The movement from process talk into more formalised oral and written reporting will need scaffolding for some EAL learners. The task is more challenging as it requires enhanced cognitive processing, as well as a more sophisticated application of language. The TA encourages the use of exploratory talk, recasting language to introduce more cognitive and academic language. They use probing questions like these:

Why do you think longer propellers make the helicopter fly better?

Which variable makes the most difference?

In developing the pupils' theories, they encourage experimentation with chunks of language that is more presentational in style, bridging the gap between oracy and literacy. Graphic organisers may help some learners organise ideas prior to more formal writing.

Quadrant C – Writing about a previous event may lack some of the context that helps EAL pupils in their learning. Thinking around a subject and extrapolating ideas is also quite abstract and consequently more difficult. In preparation for writing, some EAL learners will benefit from access to lists of appropriate vocabulary. Finally, a writing frame may help in the organisation and sequencing of the different elements of the piece.

A sample of the conclusion written by the advanced EAL learner is shown on p. 38. While it demonstrates characteristic EAL developmental features in terms of insecure use of past tense agreement, pluralisation and use of articles, it is a cohesive piece of writing showing good understanding, with appropriate use of academic vocabulary.

...To make it fair test we had to keep all the variables the same except one, which we changed each time.

We found out that a number of different variable [sic] affect the rate at which the helicopter falls to the ground. These include shape of helicopter, total mass of the helicopter, surface area of the propeller, angle of the propeller.

We discover [sic] that when the surface area of the propellers was large the time taken to fall was longer. We also noticed if they were too small or large for the body it did not fly well. This is like a sycmore [sic] seed which has wings same size as body.

To summarise, the Cummins Framework supports planning because it allows a practitioner to match the context and cognitive challenge of any activity to the needs of the learner. Crucially, it predicts the level of support required to lead an EAL learner from BICS to CALP, from quadrants A through to C. Remember that no activities should be in quadrant D!

The linguistic challenge

Overcoming the language demands embedded within learning activities is the perennial difficulty for EAL learners. Scaffolding support for EAL learners requires careful planning and necessitates much more thought than simply offering an academic word list or a few starter sentences. Any particular learning activity is likely to require sufficient language to:

- understand the nature of the task
- access oral input from the practitioner
- listen to / read and internalise curriculum-related information
- take part in whole-class / peer discussion
- complete the task in an oral or written fashion
- comprehend assessment feedback – oral or written.

In thinking about language demands, some practitioners have found planning templates useful, such as the example below.

Curriculum objectives	Key activities	Language functions	Language features	Language structures	Academic vocabulary
Desired outcomes	What will be done by learners	Techniques required in use of language	Tone, style, voice figurative language, grammar	Examples of sentence starters, linking words, etc.	Context-related words

Pro forma adapted from Teaching bilingual children in the primary years: http://nationalstrategies.standards.dcsf.gov.uk.node/85322   © Crown copyright 2006.

Language demands – a KS2 geography activity

In the next example groups of pupils have been set the task of planning and delivering a weather forecast to their peers. The completed planning pro forma below details some of the more immediate language demands placed upon EAL learners in preparing and delivering their presentation.

Curriculum objectives	Key activities	Language functions	Language features	Language structures	Academic vocabulary
To research, draft and present a weather forecast, supported by visual aids	Listening to TV and radio weather forecasts Reading weather reports in papers / on internet		Informal style Use of future tense, e.g. will	Conditional, e.g. If ... then ...	Weather terms, e.g. N, S, E, W; front, system, depression, pressure, temperature, humidity, pollen count
	Compare differences between oral and written versions	Compare	Superlatives, e.g. coldest, wettest, highest	Comparison, e.g. It will be colder/ wetter than ...	
	Drafting Making notes	Describe, explain, justify	Descriptive language, e.g. beautiful, amazing, wonderful, miserable	Cause and effect, e.g. because, so that, therefore; resulting in, creating, causing	
	Oral presentation	Predict	Modal verbs, e.g. could, should, may, might	Express possibility, e.g. it is possible, likely, probable, certain that	
		Sequence		Time connectives, e.g. before, later, after, next, when, while	
			Phrasal verbs, e.g. keep on, hold up, drag on, end up, let down, put up with		
			Personification, e.g. limp on, race in, lay around, angry clouds		
	Visual aids Use of ICT				

Obviously, it would be impractical to expect practitioners to plan this level of detail into each activity. However, it is recommended that all class teachers, perhaps with their TA or bilingual practitioner, try to plan this level of detail wherever possible.

Speaking, listening, reading and writing across the curriculum

EAL learners, at all stages in their development of English, will benefit from teaching that involves sequences of activities which naturally link the four strands of English together.

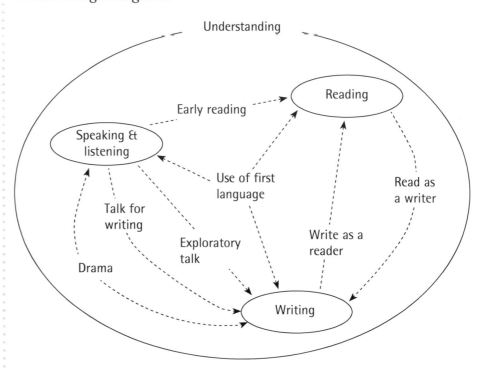

Useful resource

NALDIC ITTSEAL 'EAL learning in curriculum areas' web pages are resources that exemplify how practitioners can support literacy development in different curriculum areas: http://www.naldic.org. uk/ITTSEAL2/teaching/ ealncsubjects.cfm

Practitioners need to recognise the uneven language profiles of EAL learners who may be at different stages of development in the four strands. In addition, difficulties for EAL learners are compounded because each curriculum area utilises different registers and genres, as well as functions that require use of specific language structures and vocabulary. Planning will need to take into account the next steps for every learner and the most appropriate scaffold to support the development of oracy and literacy.

Developing speaking and listening

Learner talk may be very superficial – particularly colloquial talk, which is the main feature of group/collaborative work. EAL learners will gain a lot more from talk that allows them to extend their thinking through more constructive dialogue. This kind of exploratory talk is not likely to happen by chance. Either it is facilitated by an adult, or it emerges in situations where ground rules have been clearly laid out for the pupils, usually where participants have been given clearly identified roles.

Making process talk exploratory

Example from a Year-5 mathematics session
Transcript taken from DfES, *Excellence and Enjoyment: Learning and Teaching for Bilingual Children in the Primary Years*, DVD Section 3. © Crown copyright 2006.

Whole-class introduction

In the whole-class introduction the class teacher reminds all the pupils about listening skills, how to construct exploratory talk by modelling sentence starters and the use of appropriate connectives. They also reinforce the importance of each pupil undertaking a specific role during group work.

Teacher: What we are going to do today is that we are going to solve a mathematical problem. OK, within your groups … and I want you to remember what we have just spoken about, about giving reasons. You are going to look at the language structures you have got up on the wall *[examples of oral prompts]* that you used before really well. I also want you to be able to use these language structures *[holding up written examples on a sheet of paper]*. I want you to be able to tell the people on your table whether you agree with them or disagree with them. If you disagree with them, I would like you to give your reason … and I would also like you to be able to tell people if you have changed your mind because they have given you a good reason.

Guiding exploratory talk in a small-group situation

The teacher has chosen to work with a specific group that has been deliberately set up with EAL learners from the same language background so that they can talk together in their first language. Non-EAL learners exhibiting strong oral English skills have also been included in the group so that they can model effective use of language to their EAL peers. The teacher explains the mathematical task. Pupils are required to come up with as many four-digit number plates as possible using the digits 1,2 ,3 and 4; each digit may be used once only. Pupils are initially paired up to talk about the problem, and the teacher reinforces that the pupils may use any language they want to do their learning.

This exemplar is taken from a mathematics session built around the concept of number plates, using the digits 1, 2, 3 and 4, where each digit may be used once only. Using whole-class teaching and a guided oral session, the class teacher encourages learners to use exploratory talk to theorise about how many different combinations are possible.

Next the teacher clarifies that the pupils have understood the task by trying out a sample of different number plate examples.

T = Class teacher
P1 = Advanced EAL learner

T: I wonder, if I came up with … *[holds up a mini-whiteboard with the digits 1, 1, 2, 3 on it, and using a probing question].* Why couldn't that be one of our number plates?
P1: It couldn't be one of our number plates because you can't use more than one number on one number plate.
T: *[pause. not letting them get away with a weak answer, although they probably know what P1 meant]* We can't *[own emphasis]* use more than one number … *[pause, giving space for P1 to respond]*
P1: You can't use the same, one of same number on the same number plate.
T: Excellent, well done, I have repeated one of the digits *[recasting with the word 'digit']* and in the problem it said we can use each digit once only. Well done *[referring to P1]*, I really liked the way you used that sentence and the reason you gave. Excellent.

This short example demonstrates a number of important points about supporting the development of oral language:

- ● development of a rich, multilingual learning environment

- ● use of talk frames to model effective use of oral language

- ● paired talk as a prelude to small-group or whole-class discussion

- ● creating groups with same language EAL learners and strong English speaking role-models

- ● practitioner use of probing questions to elicit meaningful responses from learners

- ● recasting correct use of language to a learner as a way of communicating errors in oral language – for example, seamless replacement of the word 'number' with the more academic word 'digit'

- ● effective use of AfL techniques within oral feedback.

Talk for writing

This approach to developing writing focuses on encouraging learners to think and talk through their ideas and the ideas of others before writing. It allows pupils the opportunity to rehearse aspects of their writing such as structure, tone and style before the actual event. For EAL learners, particularly emergent writers, it helps to make their ideas more explicit. Talk for writing is more about the cohesiveness of writing than the use of specific vocabulary or grammatical form and, for this reason, can happen as easily in a pupil's first language as in English. Of course, this kind of talk is a process and at some point a learner will need to transfer their thinking across to English.

Some schools have a rolling programme of response partners for all learners and make explicit the expectations of the dual roles of acting as a listener or a speaker. For those newer to English, groups of three may be especially useful as the EAL learner can hear both sides of the conversation modelled, joining in when confident enough to do so.

EAL learners within early years settings

Here are some suggestions for practitioners who are working with children learning EAL to support understanding and develop oral language:

- ● use of visual aids – for example, pictorial timelines showing the sequence of daily activities

- ● use of body gestures, facial expressions and change in voice to enhance meaning

- ● ensuring that EAL learners have the chance to watch and hear other children take their turn first in group activities, so that they can copy them

- ● allowing more time for children learning EAL to respond

- ● development of activities that encourage repetition of language

- ● use of visual/sound resources to mark the transition between activities throughout the day – for example, photographs, smiley faces, music

Useful resource

DCSF (2007) Supporting children learning English as an additional language: guidance for practitioners in the Early Years Foundation Stage: http://nationalstrategies. standards.dcsf.gov.uk/primary/ publications/foundation_stage/ eal_eyfs/

○ oral interaction between practitioners and children in formal and social situations

○ allocating non-verbal tasks to EAL learners – for example, giving out snacks/equipment.

Creating opportunities for speaking and listening

Activities might include:

○ play-based learning

○ story-telling

○ drama and role-play

○ practical investigations in mathematics, science and technology

○ ICT-based activities – for example, multimedia books, podcasting

○ games-based activities (see below).

Games are a great way to generate interaction and oral communication between peers. It is easy to apply content within any curriculum area to board/card games, dominoes, snakes and ladders, quizzes, and so on. Practitioners can make games for learners and there is also potential for pupils to make games for each other. Barrier games are particularly good for developing both colloquial and academic language. Here, two peers, or a pupil and an adult practitioner, sit astride a physical barrier. Each player possesses an incomplete resource such as a map or diagram, and the task is for each player to collaborate with the other by asking questions in order to complete their own version.

Games-based activities within the curriculum are beneficial because:

○ they are fun and encourage natural socialisation

○ they have a strong visual element

○ the concept is usually culturally familiar, even if the specific games are not

○ oral language is developed in a real context

○ playing them involves repetition of similar language structures and vocabulary

○ pupils learn curriculum content without realising.

Developing reading

The teaching of reading to all learners needs to include a combination of techniques. Activating prior knowledge is the first step, with whole-class teaching and modelling, small-group guided sessions supported by a practitioner, and opportunities for independent reading with peers or family members.

Useful resources for speaking and listening

Digital story-telling: http://www.segfl.org.uk/emas/storytelling

Talk for writing: http://nationalstrategies.standards.dcsf.gov.uk/node/154519

Teachers' TV 'Talk and EAL at Green End Primary': http://www.teachers.tv/video/30990

Beware ...

of being misled by EAL learners who decode well and read at pace. Some may have poor comprehension skills.

Food for thought

Some EAL learners read at an age-appropriate level in their first language, but not in English.

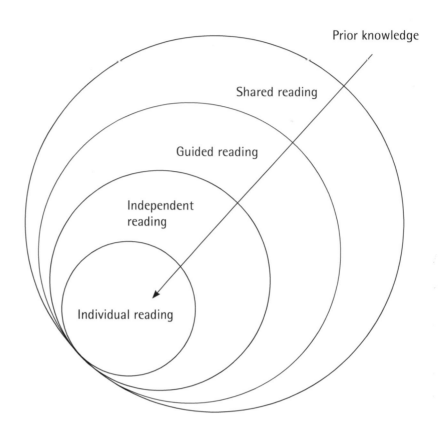

An approach to a reading sequence could involve any, or all, of the above activities.

Some issues to consider:

- The ability of some EAL learners to decode words can mask their general ability to interpret and fully comprehend a text. Some learners arrive from abroad having been effectively taught to 'bark at print' without having any real understanding of what they are reading.

- Try to avoid teaching reading too early – for example, before a learner has sufficient oral 'pegs' upon which to hang phonemes and word recognition. This is particularly important for older beginner EAL learners who have limited or no literacy in their first language, as they will have very little phonemic awareness to transfer across to learning of English.

Texts used with all learners need to be free from negative cultural bias. Where possible, use texts that are reflective of the linguistic, cultural and religious heritages of the target EAL learners. This will enhance pupil motivation, self-esteem and comprehension. Pupils who are literate in their first language will benefit from access to dual-language texts; this will enable learners to transfer knowledge of literacy across languages, supporting the development of reading in English.

Here are some ideas for developing reading with EAL learners:

- Build upon prior knowledge, including where possible reading skills and strategies used in the first language.

- Employ a range of reading opportunities – shared, guided and individual sessions.

- Develop effective questioning techniques to extend pupils' understanding of texts.

- Use age-appropriate material to teach reading.

- Teach phonics, when necessary, within a clear context such as a familiar book.

- Utilise multisensory approaches through the use of story props and other artefacts.

- Use talking books as this will help cement knowledge of sound–letter correspondence and word recognition.

- Employ screen-reading software to enhance a learner's access to text. This is particularly beneficial for EAL learners who have stronger oracy than literacy.

- Utilise the interactive whiteboard for shared reading activities.

- Develop text-marking activities, in which learners highlight incidences of specific use of language in a text.

- Use Directed Activities Related to Texts (DARTs) – for example, cloze procedures, sequencing activities, 'top and tail' sentences, organising text into topic sentences, transferring information from prose to tables and vice versa.

Developing writing

In general, writing presents a bigger challenge for EAL learners than speaking; this is true of both beginner and advanced EAL learners, although the specific barriers and difficulties will obviously be different. The table over the page illustrates some of the reasons why writing is significantly more difficult than speaking and offers some helpful support strategies.

Aspects that pose difficulty	Suggested support strategies
Distance. Speech has an immediate context, where meaning is usually obvious and information can be conveyed visually. Writing tends to be separated from context by time and space.	• Embed writing tasks around events that have well-established meaning for the learner – e.g. a family event; a school visit; show and tell; a bilingual, culturally appropriate text (supported orally if necessary). • Allow learners time to talk with peers in preparation for writing.
Cues. As well as the actual words used in speech, talk also conveys meaning through other oral cues such as intonation, stress, pitch, volume, pace, etc. Writing has a smaller range of cues.	• Model use of genres / text types through shared and guided writing sessions. • Provide specific examples of writing – e.g. different genres and voices
Organising content. Writing tasks may require a learner to order, synthesise, categorise and re-purpose large amounts of information prior to writing. Text may also need formatting in particular ways.	• Mind maps are useful for showing the connectedness of ideas and language – their visual nature supports understanding and memorisation of information. • Graphic organisers help EAL learners categorise information and organise thoughts in preparation for writing – they help break tasks down into manageable steps. • Writing fames help learners to structure their writing – e.g. headings, paragraphing, starter sentences and chunks of text which are connected by logical relationships. Note that you should avoid overuse of writing frames, especially with advanced learners, as it may restrict creativity.
Cohesion. Some EAL writers, particularly beginners, struggle to write cohesively because they lack, or are still developing, markers that make text predictable and coherent – e.g. appropriate use of connectives, consistent use of tense and person, referential use of pronouns and articles.	• For beginner EAL learners, encourage risk-taking and avoid overcorrection of spelling and grammar. • Develop collaborative text reconstruction activities; oral interaction with peers may be in English or first language. • Word-processors can speed up the writing process – teach effective use of tools such as spelling/grammar check, thesaurus. • Use of supportive word-processors – e.g. Cricksoft's Clicker and Write Online.
Complexity. Writing tends to use longer statements with more sophisticated and precise vocabulary.	• Encourage oral rehearsal, especially of more formal language. • Word mats and vocabulary lists help with subject-specific language. • Translated word lists, bilingual dictionaries and translation engines can be useful for EAL learners literate in first language.
Delayed feedback. Oral work usually provides learners with immediate feedback – e.g. facial expressions, nodding. Feedback on writing may be delayed or may happen only after the final version.	• Ensure adequate time for drafting. • Encourage reading of drafts aloud. • Enable opportunities for peer assessment. • Provide practitioner support for checking of first and subsequent drafts.

Resources to support writing

Clicker and Write Online from Cricksoft: www.cricksoft.com

Case study

Planning for a persuasive writing task

In a geography unit of work on local traffic movement, a Year-5 class had researched the pros and cons of a council proposal to build a tram system through their town. One aspect of the council's proposal involved the destruction of a local skateboard park. The class teacher decided to dovetail this work with a persuasive writing task. Pupils were asked to draft persuasive letters to the council to stop its proposed destruction of the skateboard park.

The sequence of activities below demonstrates one way of preparing pupils for the writing task.

> **Research from geography unit – information from a real context supports EAL learners' understanding and develops academic vocabulary for this persuasive writing task.**

> Shared-reading session using a modelled text – persuasive letters written by peers from previous years. Examples make the task explicit for EAL learners.
>
> Looking at the features of persuasive texts supports grammar for writing and how to develop a persuasive text type. Focus on sentence-level activities.

> Independent writing – small-group collaborative development of a PowerPoint presentation and notes for presentation.
>
> Talk for writing.

> Guided-reading session – the group analyses samples of other persuasive writing – e.g. direct mail marketing, charity leaflets, letters in the news, web pages/ blogs.

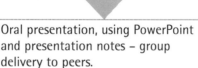

> Oral presentation, using PowerPoint and presentation notes – group delivery to peers.
>
> Consolidation of academic vocabulary and persuasive techniques helps support the writing process.

> Individual writing – pupils draft letters to the local council urging them to avoid the destruction of the skateboard park or to build a new one.
>
> PowerPoint notes/slides help organise ideas and stage the writing task.
>
> Possible use of writing frame and information and communication technology (ICT) to support writing.

In the example above, EAL learners benefit from:
- modelling of persuasive texts through shared- and guided-reading sessions
- building upon prior learning from work in a geography topic – this provides a more concrete context for the task
- collaborative group work where talk is central to learning – preparation of PowerPoint and presentation notes
- oral presentation – this helps model more formal use of persuasive language
- referring back to the PowerPoint presentation and notes to support the final persuasive writing task.

Useful resources

More detailed advice and guidance about developing speaking, listening, reading and writing for EAL learners may be found in Unit 2 of Teaching bilingual children in the primary years: http://nationalstrategies.standards.dcsf.gov.uk/node/88159

DfES (2003) Assessment in mathematics: toolkit to support pupils for whom English is an additional language: http://nationalstrategies.standards.dcsf.gov.uk/node/154719

Food for thought

Some EAL learners outperform their white British monolingual peers in English, yet underperform in mathematics.

The language of mathematics

While mathematics is said to be an international language at which EAL learners can compete on an equal footing with their peers, there is concern nationally about the underattainment of some EAL learners. This situation may be replicated in your own local contexts (local authority or school).

Here are some issues to consider:

❍ Some languages have alternative number scripts with which EAL learners may be more familiar – for example, this Bengali number line:

৹ ১ ২ ৩ ৪ ৫ ৬ ৭ ৮ ৯ ১৹

Some adjustment may be necessary in moving to the Hindu-Arabic number system used in the UK.

❍ In some countries the use of mathematical symbols may be different – for example, a multiplication symbol can look like a decimal point between two numbers, so that 2.6 means 2 x 6.

❍ Try using EAL learners' experience of other number scripts in lessons. This can allow those pupils to become the 'experts' and contributes to the overall intercultural dimension of the curriculum.

❍ Pupils who have learned mathematics abroad may have missed some aspects of a traditional UK maths curriculum. However, they may be more proficient in other areas – for example, algebra and trigonometry.

❍ Ways of solving numerical problems vary from country to country and some pupils will not be comfortable with considering different approaches as they have been taught to rely on one solution. However, different methods from other countries can be used as interesting teaching points. In addition, if a pupil has a secure method they should not be dissuaded from using it just because it does not conform to more standard methods. The example below shows a method for multiplication that was popular in India and is still taught today in some places.

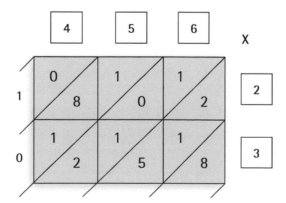

Gelosia multiplication method

One of the difficulties of the UK mathematics curriculum is that it is very verbose. Despite having competence in many mathematical areas, some EAL learners struggle to demonstrate their true ability. Knowledge of vocabulary and grammar is one of the keys to success. The wordy nature of problems may present cultural challenges for those learners educated abroad, as the contexts tend to be central to understanding the nature of the problem.

Here are some ways of tackling the language demands of mathematics:

- Utilise pictorial, graphical and written models for solving problems.
- Create plenty of speaking and listening opportunities, especially to scaffold different types of sentence structure.
- Use oral prompt resources – for example, number/word fans, reasoning sentence starters.
- Break complex problems down into stages: chunk the word problem and link with the individual mathematical operators.
- Show the multitude of words and phrases associated with the four numerical operators – for example, x, multiply, times, product.
- Make specific reference to homonyms – words that look and sound the same but have mathematical meaning as well as a more literary one – for example, root, power, mean, table.
- Use ICT creatively – for example, interactive whiteboards and RM Easiteach software.

Use of ICT

For EAL learners, it is particularly important to embed the use of ICT across the curriculum: an overemphasis on discrete teaching of ICT skills will usually lack the all-important context needed for learning. ICT thus becomes a tool to support learning rather than being the learning itself. Wegerif (2004) has written about the significance of ICT in developing exploratory talk, and it is recommended that EAL learners generally work in pairs or small groups when engaged in ICT.

The benefits of ICT include:

- multimodality – text, audio, visual, kinaesthetic learning
- support for developing understanding, speaking, listening, reading and writing
- facility for self-paced learning
- opportunity for repetition and rehearsal
- continuity and progression in learning
- enabling use of first language to support learning.

Resources

Collaborative Learning Project – mathematics activities http://www.collaborativelearning.org/mathsonline.html

Useful resources

TTS – Easi-Speak microphones: www.tts-group.co.uk
2Simple – 2Create A Story: http://www.2simpleshop.com/2createastory
Mantra Lingua's Recordable TalkingPEN: www.mantralingua.com/pages.php?pageid=16
Google Earth: http://earth.google.com/
Cricksoft's Clicker 5: www.cricksoft.com/uk/products/clicker
Babel Fish: http://uk.babelfish.yahoo.com

More examples of good practice may be accessed on NALDIC's Youtube website: ICT and EAL Vodcasts – http://www.youtube.com/view_play_list?p=C51EA34FA5807FF6

Some examples of using ICT across the curriculum are shown below.

AU = Curriculum access and understanding
SL = Speaking and listening
R = Reading   W = Writing

Example	AU	SL	R	W
As part of continuous provision in a Year R class, a role-play area had been set up as a TV and radio station. Some pupils decided to interview and record their peers and some adults about their families using Easi-Speak microphones. One of the EAL learners in the class was able to interview a bilingual mother in her own first language. Recordings of interviews were used by the class teacher for AfL purposes and backed up on a computer. The EAL learners benefited from the focus on oracy and the opportunity to have their ability in their first language validated.	✓	✓		
During a topic on 'Our World', a Year-1 class used 2Simple's 2Create A Story software to produce a multimedia story about their locality. After teacher input, the pupils worked in pairs to discuss their theme. Working together, they drew pictures and animated them, wrote some accompanying text and added an oral narrative using microphones. With the help of a bilingual practitioner, some of the EAL learners were able to add an oral component in their first language. The use of multimedia helped all learners, particularly EAL learners, to make meaning explicit.	✓	✓	✓	✓
A Year-2 class used Mantra Lingua's TalkingPEN and recordable stickers in a series of numeracy sessions to make board games based on numerical operators. In small groups they designed the game, made the boards and created extra resources such as quiz cards. They also wrote the rules for playing the game. Using the pen and stickers, they recorded oral content such as instructions for what to do when a player lands on a game square or quiz questions and answers. Finally they swapped games so another group could have a go at playing them. The EAL learners benefited from the collaborative approach and the focus on oracy, and from being able to use the technology to record and hear recordings repetitively.	✓	✓	✓	✓
A Year-3 new-arrival EAL learner, from Turkey, used Google Earth on a classroom computer during morning registration. Over the course of one week he worked with his class buddy and a TA to explore his country of origin and look at photographs of some familiar places. The group also looked at the school locality within the wider context of the UK. The focus on oracy really suited this beginner EAL learner.	✓	✓		
When a British-born, Year-4 Bangladeshi girl went on a three-month visit to her parents' home in the Sylhet area, she took lots of digital pictures and kept a diary. On her return she used Clicker 5 to produce a bilingual talking book about her trip. This was subsequently showcased to the whole of the class via the interactive whiteboard. Not only did the activity celebrate her own culture, but it provided a real context that allowed her to develop literacy in both languages.		✓	✓	✓
During a G&T after-school club, a group of Year-5 learners worked on producing a DVD aimed at new arrivals. The group of white British and EAL learners was supported by a school-based TA and a peripatetic bilingual practitioner. The pupils scripted, filmed and cut the DVD themselves, and bilingual learners in the group were able to dub over the video with oral narrations in a range of different languages. The collaborative nature of the task, the integration of speaking, listening, reading and writing, and the use of first language and ICT supported all the learners.	✓	✓	✓	✓
A Year-6 new-arrival Spanish-speaking pupil was supported in class by a TA during literacy sessions. In order to access text and key tasks, the beginner EAL learner and the TA worked together to translate keywords using an online English–Spanish translation engine (Babel Fish). The oral discussion between TA and learner was very supportive and use of the technology enabled transfer of knowledge and skills from their first language to the learning of English.	✓	✓	✓	✓

Demonstrating achievement

One of the biggest challenges for practitioners working with EAL learners is how to demonstrate progression in learning. When thinking about the range of EAL learners in our schools it should be recognised that it is not realistic, or even desirable, to expect a formal written outcome continually, especially from beginner EAL learners. However, there are many other ways for learners to demonstrate learning:

- physical responses that demonstrate understanding – for example, following instructions, facial expression, gesture

- annotated drawings

- completion of charts/diagrams/maps/tables

- use of traffic-light cards where red = don't understand, amber = not sure, green = understand – particularly useful for oral work

- feedback via a peer talk-partner or bilingual practitioner

- oral recording – for example, via digital microphone/dictaphone, Mantra Lingua's Recordable TalkingPEN

- photographic records

- short video clips

- writing in first language.

Chapter 4
Interventions and strategies for schools to employ

This chapter is all about how to target intervention for the individual needs of EAL learners most effectively. It considers different approaches to intervention, both within and external to mainstream classroom teaching, using the expertise of additional adults. The first part of the chapter focuses on the induction and settlement of new-arrival BME/EAL learners. The rest of the chapter looks at some specific intervention programmes as well as at how to develop successful bespoke withdrawal sessions.

Catering for the needs of new arrivals

New-arrival EAL learners seem to give schools a disproportionate amount of worry. However, the reality is that most new arrivals will settle quickly and make rapid progress as long as they are inducted effectively and taught inclusively.

A whole-school approach

Provision for EMA is a whole-school issue, but it is particularly important that all staff understand their role in inducting and assessing new arrivals, as well as in the provision for those at the early stages of learning English. Key staff include the administration team, class teacher, bilingual staff, ethnic minority coordinator and TAs who may be involved in specialist provision for learners of EAL. In addition, some EAL learners have SEN and therefore the school's SEN team would also be involved to meet their needs.

Preparation for new arrivals and first contact with the pupil and family

Where possible, schools need to prepare actively for the arrival of BME/EAL learners. As we all know from past experience, first impressions can make a huge difference to relationships for a long time afterwards. You may like to use the photocopiable checklist on p. 57 to help with your planning.

Here are some practical suggestions for the whole school community:

- ○ Ensure a welcoming environment for pupils and their families – more on this in Chapter 5.
- ○ Identify sources of bilingual practitioners – for example, the local authority or community.
- ○ Purchase a range of bilingual dictionaries for the library.
- ○ Ensure the family has copies of the school prospectus (including a translation if possible).

- Check the accuracy of initial details – for example, names, year group, ethnicity.

- Prepare the class for the arrival of a new pupil – perhaps research some facts about country background, learn some basic words and phrases in their first language.

- Identify a number of pupils to act as buddies to the new pupil – it can be useful to use someone from the same language background, but it is a good strategy to use pupils from a range of backgrounds, including white British children.

- Provide the pupil and family with a tour of the school.

- Introduce the pupil and family to key staff.

Induction – the first week

New pupils will really appreciate a structured introduction to the school in their first week. This will enable them to settle and get a feel for an educational environment that may be culturally very different from what they have been used to in their country of origin. From the school's perspective this is also an important opportunity to begin the assessment process.

Here are some suggested activities for pupil induction:

- Ensure the new pupil is supported by a peer buddy throughout the day, especially during breaks and lunchtimes.

- Provide the new learner with a visual timetable and talk it through with them – even if the pupil has come with a good grasp of English there are likely to be socio-cultural barriers, such as subjects that the learner has never studied before.

- Check that the learner has the correct uniform and all the equipment needed for lessons.

- Introduce the pupil to the workings of the library and register them in the system.

- Give the pupil their network log-in details and ensure that they know the procedure for logging on to the school network – an introduction to the main features of the school's virtual learning environment / learning platform would be beneficial for most learners, unless ICT is a completely new experience for them.

- Encourage EAL learners who are literate in their first language to bring their own bilingual dictionary or borrow one from the library (where possible).

- Beginner EAL learners will also benefit from 'survival' language visual dictionaries and word fans – showing words or phrases that a learner may need to communicate but is unable to manage owing to lack of language.

The next steps

Within the first couple of weeks it is essential to hold a parent conference in order to gather important information about the new pupil (see p. 54).

In addition, a full assessment of the learner's ability across the curriculum is needed to inform effective teaching and learning provision – this has been covered in detail in Chapter 2.

The initial interview / parent conference

One of the most important elements of the pupil induction process is the opportunity to talk with parents and carers alongside their child. During a parent conference, it is possible to obtain critical background information about the whole family. You should also find out about the pupil's previous educational experience, general ability, skills and aptitudes, and other miscellaneous details that help create a more rounded picture of them. Schools that handle new-arrival induction successfully tend to have a dedicated member of staff or small team to organise and conduct induction, including parent conferencing.

Providing bilingual interpreters

It is often necessary to organise a bilingual interpreter for parent conferences. Some schools employ their own bilingual practitioners. It may be possible to utilise a pool of experienced interpreters from the local authority. Family friends and older siblings could assist with interpreting. Parents of other children at the school may be prepared to help with interpreting on a casual basis, and some schools even use older pupils within the school, particularly those who have been trained through, for example, young interpreting schemes (see Chapter 5). Obviously some information is very personal, possibly confidential, so care needs to be taken about what questions are asked through interpreters who are pupils or parents of other children in the school. Some bilingual adults may know the family or relatives in the community. This is worth establishing from the outset as it may govern the range of potential questions. It is also worth double-checking the language spoken as some languages have dialectal forms that can make communication much harder.

Preparation and conducting the interview – some general points:

- ◗ Contact parents/carers to explain the purpose of the meeting – use an interpreter where necessary.

- ◗ Try to brief the interpreter prior to the meeting and show them any pro forma that may be used (see photocopiables on pp. 55 and 56).

- ◗ Set the room up as naturally and informally as possible.

- ◗ When communicating through an interpreter, direct questions at the parents, maintain eye contact and use plenty of non-verbal gestures.

Online background collation tool for new arrivals: http://newarrivals.segfl.org.uk

Finding interpreters for parent conferencing may sometimes prove difficult. Some practitioners use an online tool to gather all the relevant background information. Questions within the tool are available in the first language with additional audio support. The questionnaire requires a user to tick boxes, with a minimal amount of additional typing. Once completed, the finished questionnaire is emailed to the user.

New arrivals – background information

Personal and family details

Full name:

Preferred name:

Class:

Class teacher:

Gender:

M   F

Date of birth:

Country of origin:

Date of arrival in UK:

Religion:

Ethnicity:

Refugee status:

Father/carer name:

Mother/carer name:

Siblings:

Current address:

Emergency contact:

Translator/interpreter needs of family:

Dietary issues:

Medical conditions:

Religious requirements:

Any known specific cognitive/developmental issues?

New arrivals – background information
(cont.)

Previous education

Age started school:

Number of years' schooling:

Time missed / repeated years:

Best/Worst subjects in country of origin:

Number of years studying English:

Subjects that pupil has never studied:

Pupil skills/abilities

First language:

Is pupil interested in continuing to learn first language at a community language school?

| Yes | No | More info needed |

Languages (include first language)	Speak	Read	Write	When/For what purpose is the language used?

Detail any particular skills/abilities/interests (e.g. curriculum-related, sport, music, art, cultural, religious)

Checklist for new-arrival EAL learners

When	Type of provision/action	Sign & date
Before arrival	Develop relevant language/cultural classroom and corridor displays	
	Talk to the class about the arrival of a new pupil – e.g. discuss country of origin, languages spoken	
	Prepare early-language support pack – e.g. picture/word fans, basic phrases	
On first day	Parent conference arranged/conducted	
	Tour of school arranged and introduction to key staff	
	Handbook given to parents – key elements translated where necessary	
	Where possible, identify bilingual adult and/or peer to assist with interpreting/translation	
In first week	Parent conference conducted and information disseminated to key staff	
	Ensure pupil has correct uniform/equipment	
	Identify a class buddy – e.g. from same language background	
	Visual timetable developed for pupil	
	Bilingual dictionary available for classroom use, where appropriate	
In first two weeks	First-language assessment conducted	
	Initial assessment of English, mathematics and use of ICT	
	Observations of learning across the curriculum	
	Early profile developed	
	Set language targets for the learner or develop an ILP	
	Identify and implement specific interventions where appropriate – e.g. pre-teaching sessions, guided writing sessions, talking partners, one-to-one tuition	
	Ensure grouping for learner meets cognitive and academic potential rather than level of English	
Within first half-term	Review meeting, with parents/carers – progress against targets – social integration	

NAEP CPD modules
http://nationalstrategies.
standards.dcsf.gov.uk/
node/113690

NAEP e-Learning course
http://nationalstrategies.
standards.dcsf.gov.uk/
node/164071

NAEP guidance booklet,
pp. 60–67: http://
nationalstrategies.standards.
dcsf.gov.uk/node/97335

**Other useful resources
for induction,
assessment and early
profiling**
QCA Pathways to Learning
for New Arrivals: http://www.
qcda.gov.uk/7526.aspx

Customisable family learning
booklets about the UK
education system:
http://microsites.segfl.org.uk/
view_page.php?id=601

Mantra Lingua: http://www.
matralingua.com
Welcome booklet CD-Rom

Paramount Education: http://
www.mynewschool.biz/index.
php
My New School: induction,
inclusion and assessment pack

Continuing professional development and self-evaluation

The DCSF New Arrivals Excellence Programme (NAEP) contains specific training modules for use with all staff or selected groups. The materials are self-contained, with briefing notes for facilitators, details of activities and photocopiable sheets. The modules may be delivered as a series or used more flexibly to suit each school's situation.

There is also an e-learning module that individuals can work through at their own pace; it is particularly suited to practitioners who are new to working with beginner EAL learners.

Included within the NAEP general guidance booklet is a self-evaluation matrix that is useful for senior leaders to use in order to collate evidence about the school's support for new-arrival BME/EAL learners.

To withdraw or not to withdraw?

This is the BIG question! The first thing to say is that the vast majority of a pupil's learning should take place in the classroom through quality-first teaching and a range of guided sessions supported by a practitioner. Withdrawal of an EAL learner from the classroom should never be a substitute for learning that should take place in the classroom. Intervention should be a genuine response to the identification of a particular language-related need that has become apparent through ongoing assessment for learning in the mainstream classroom. Where intervention is necessary, careful planning needs to ensure that every session is planned in advance, has a clear rationale, is linked to the curriculum and is time limited.

When organising withdrawal intervention sessions, do:

- ◑ think carefully about when to withdraw; try to avoid hitting the same curriculum slots, practical activities or situations in which EAL learners can contribute on an equal footing, such as modern foreign languages

- ◑ link work directly to the curriculum rather than offering de-contextualised content

- ◑ focus work on specific language targets

- ◑ try to teach learners in pairs or small groups

- ◑ create opportunities to use oracy as a springboard to developing literacy

- ◑ use age-appropriate, cognitively challenging texts when teaching reading

- ◑ avoid teaching phonics to beginner EAL learners who don't have sufficient oracy as they will not have adequate vocabulary upon which to hang their phonetic learning.

Here are some appropriate activities for withdrawal sessions:

- ◑ involvement in a recommended strategy intervention

- new-arrival induction and orientation

- grammatical focus to plug specific gaps in an advanced learner's repertoire

- early literacy intervention for older beginner EAL learners who have limited or no literacy in their first language

- pre-teaching of key vocabulary with visual support and explanation of concepts for upcoming lessons

- post-teaching – recap and consolidation

- specific short-term project based on skills and interests of target pupil(s) – for example, digital story-telling, making talking books, research-based activities

- fun-based activities where oracy and repetition are central to learning – for example, card/board games, barrier games (see Chapter 3)

- enrichment activities – for example, out-of-school visits

- limited, short-burst use of ICT programmes to learn English – for example, Clicker Beginner English, Success Maker Discover English, Rosetta Stone, Eurotalk.

Specialist interventions

Talking partners

This is a well-established talk-centred intervention initially developed in Bradford for use with EAL learners. The approach enables learners to articulate their ideas about reading and rehearses vocabulary, grammar and syntax orally, before commencing writing. The success of Talking Partners is evidenced by the fact that many schools have trained practitioners and use the approach with all kinds of learners.

Talking partners:

- focuses on the centrality of talk in learning

- works best as an initiative to develop literacy across the curriculum

- is an intensive ten-week course with groups of three children supported by one trained adult

- is most usually organised as three 20-minute sessions per week

- utilises materials and strategies taken from the curriculum being taught in the classroom at the time.

Teaching units to support writing in EAL

These pilot materials for guided sessions are designed to be used by a trained adult working with small groups of advanced EAL learners in Years 2–6. Learners need to be working at or above level 2C in writing.

One-to-one tuition

This intervention is closely related to specific gaps in learning identified through the use of APP materials. Tutoring is intended to focus on these

Beware ...

of overusing ICT-based English teaching programmes. They tend to teach language in a rather de-contextualised way. It is recommended that their use is in short bursts and time limited.

Useful resource

Talking partners: https://schools.educationbradford.com/schools/CMSPage.aspx?mid=415#Talking_Partners_Information

Find out more:

See http://nationalstrategies.standards.dcsf.gov.uk/node/88717
A range of practical literacy activities are supported by Clicker grids on an accompanying CD-Rom.

gaps in order to provide the learner with strategies that can be applied in a range of new contexts. Clearly some EAL learners will benefit from focused, personalised support that can address gaps in knowledge and clarify areas of misunderstanding. For EAL learners acquiring English, tuition should address gaps in subject knowledge and how to express that subject knowledge appropriately in English.

Here are some questions worth considering:

● Are class and subject teachers sufficiently aware of the need to assess language development for EAL learners alongside curricular learning – for example, is the gap that the pupil is demonstrating related to their subject knowledge or to how well they can currently express their understanding in English?

● Are tutors sufficiently aware of the distinctive language and learning needs of EAL learners to be able to offer appropriate support?

● Has the school effectively communicated the aims of one-to-one tuition to the parents/carers of the learner, where appropriate using translators/ interpreters?

● Has the school considered specific issues – for example, the appropriateness of using male tutors with female pupils from certain cultural backgrounds?

● Has planning factored in the additional time constraints that can impinge upon some BME pupils – for example, evening religious observance/ learning, Saturday/Sunday community language classes?

Chapter 5
Whole-school approaches

One of the key messages about developing whole-school approaches to EMA is that the most effective provision not only benefits EAL learners but the whole school population. Research by Blair and Bourne (1998) into the features of successful multi-ethnic schools identified some common themes, such as these:

- the significant role played by headteachers in driving forward an inclusive agenda

- working in partnership with parents

- establishing strong community links

- developing pupil-centred approaches to learning

- embedding robust procedures for dealing with racist incidents

- effective monitoring and tracking of pupil progress.

Provision for EMA and children learning EAL is couched firmly within the wider agenda of Every Child Matters. It will be driven by national initiatives, locally agreed targets and current focuses within the School Improvement Plan. The development of strong policies helps to ensure accountability for specific areas of work. Most importantly, catering for the needs of BME/EAL learners involves the whole school community and its relationship with the wider community.

An example of a whole-school approach to EMA

Every school organises its staffing in different ways and therefore roles and responsibilities may fall upon a variety of different shoulders. One important principle to remember is that provision for EMA and EAL learners is larger than the role of one person. Schools with good capacity understand that work needs to be distributed amongst a variety of staff – see the example on p. 62. Some staff will require specific training to undertake more specialist activities, such as new-arrival induction and assessment or work on intervention.

Some observations about organising staffing:

- It is recommended that every school appoints an EMA coordinator to oversee all aspects of the work, including managing EMA-funded staff. Where possible this person should be part of the senior leadership team (SLT).

- Some schools may choose to combine the EMA role with others – for example, an inclusion post.

- Training a full/part-time TA to fulfil specialist EMA roles helps to distribute key tasks and builds capacity.

An example of a whole-school approach to EMA

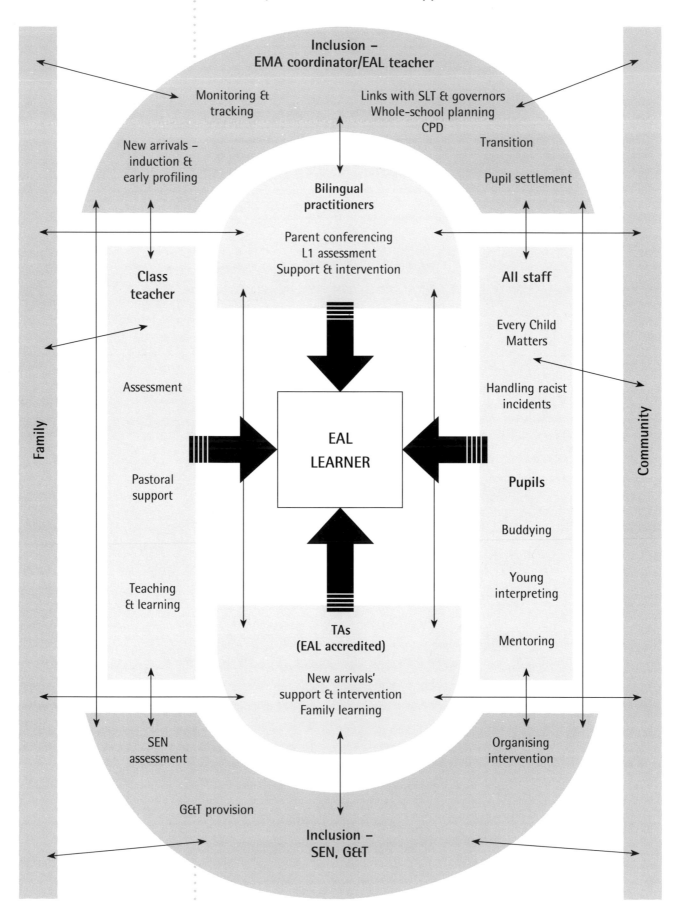

Inclusion –
EMA coordinator/EAL teacher

Monitoring &
tracking

Links with SLT & governors
Whole-school planning
CPD

New arrivals –
induction &
early profiling

Transition

Pupil settlement

Bilingual
practitioners

Parent conferencing
L1 assessment
Support & intervention

Class
teacher

All staff

Assessment

Every Child
Matters

Handling racist
incidents

EAL
LEARNER

Pastoral
support

Pupils

Family

Community

Buddying

Teaching
& learning

Young
interpreting

TAs
(EAL accredited)

Mentoring

New arrivals'
support & intervention
Family learning

SEN
assessment

Organising
intervention

G&T provision

Inclusion –
SEN, G&T

- Appointing governors from BME backgrounds will reinforce links with local communities.

- Some schools appoint full/part-time bilingual practitioners to support EAL learners from the groups comprising the largest numbers or those most in need (see below).

- All staff will need access to CPD – for example, EAL classroom strategies, diversifying the curriculum, assessment and race equality (including handling racist incidents).

- EMA-funded staff will also need access to mainstream CPD.

Working with a bilingual practitioner

Working with bilingual practitioners is key to the successful integration and achievement of EAL learners, particularly those new to English. Here are some suggestions about how to make the most effective use of bilingual practitioners:

Using your bilingual practitioner to support teaching and learning

- Find time to plan with them in order to feed their input into short-term planning.
- When there are a number of target pupils, direct them to work with the learners that meet your objectives.
- Share the learner's language targets or ILP with your bilingual practitioner.
- Avoid using them to work with pupils out of the classroom.
- Use them flexibly – e.g. 1:1 support, working with small groups.
- Provide them with a book/file and encourage them to keep a record of significant pupil achievements on a daily basis.
- Encourage them to bring in bilingual materials, cultural and religious objects, etc.
- Use their first-language skills to prepare dual language signs, keyword translations for teaching materials and classroom displays.
- Seek advice from them on the cultural/religious appropriateness of tasks.
- Talk to them at the end of each session to obtain feedback about the progress of the target pupil(s).
- Invite them to progress/review meetings for their target pupil(s).

Using your bilingual practitioner for other activities

- Use their interpreting skills during parent conferences, teacher–parent meetings and home visits.
- Use their interpreting and translating skills for first-language assessments.
- Utilise their first-language skills to translate key documents.
- Where appropriate, enable them to support pupils during internal and external examinations.
- Provide space and time for them to use the first language to communicate ongoing issues with the family.
- Invite them to accompany target pupil(s) on school trips.
- Ask them to share linguistic and cultural experience with all pupils – e.g. in curriculum time, an intercultural day, school assembly.
- Encourage them to feed back on EAL pupils' achievements within the community – e.g. progress in community language classes, religious achievements and rites of passage.

How to help your bilingual practitioner

- If they are not school-based, do show them round and introduce them to key staff.
- Find out about their background and skills; this will enable you to use them more effectively and make them feel more valued.
- Provide them with a space in which to keep personal items.
- Ensure plenty of time for them to prepare for interpreting and to undertake translation as both are very skilled activities.
- Organise a communication book so that messages can be sent backwards and forwards between them and staff.

Policy development

Developing robust policies is one of the ways to ensure effective procedures are in place to support pupils learning EAL, and to take into account the wider agenda for BME pupils. This will require the creation of separate policies, as well as the inclusion of EAL-related issues in other policies.

Suggested standalone policies should include the following:

◗ **Race equality.** The Race Relations (Amendment) Act 2000 places a general duty on local education authorities (including schools) to
- eliminate unlawful racial discrimination
- promote equal opportunities
- promote good relations between people of different racial groups.

◗ **Community cohesion.** The Education and Inspections Act 2006 places a duty on the governing bodies of all maintained schools in England to promote community cohesion and also on Ofsted to report on schools' work in this area.

◗ Inclusion – including EMA and EAL.

BME and EAL issues should also be embedded within other policies – for example, admissions, literacy, assessment, intercultural, SEN, G&T, behaviour and attendance.

The inclusive school

The effectiveness of a school's provision for BME and EAL learners is likely to be reflected in the wider apparatus of school life that encompasses the learning environment, staffing, curriculum and specific approaches to teaching and learning. These aspects are fundamentally intertwined, each one impacting on its neighbours to create a supportive culture that enables all learners to reach their full potential.

Handling racist incidents

It is recommended good practice for schools to record racist incidents. In accordance with locally agreed guidelines, schools may also be required to report the details to the local authority on a regular basis.

Approaches that many schools and practitioners find useful:

Social and Emotional Aspects of Learning (SEAL): http://nationalstrategies.standards.dcsf.gov.uk/inclusion/behaviourattendanceandseal/primaryseal

UNICEF's Rights Respecting Schools Award – http://rrsa.unicef.org.uk/

Useful resources:

QCDA – Respect for All. A website to promote diversity and challenge racism through the curriculum: http://www.qcda.gov.uk/6753.aspx

Multiverse. An initial teacher education website funded by the Teacher Development Agency to address the educational achievement of pupils from diverse backgrounds: http://www.multiverse.ac.uk

Junior European Languages Portfolio by CILT: http://www.primarylanguages.org.uk/resources/assessment_and_recording/european_languages_portfolio.aspx

iRespect . An award-winning website: http://www.irespect.net

Some important considerations:

○ All staff should have training in identifying, recording and dealing effectively with racist incidents.

○ The school's handling of racist incidents should be monitored regularly; scrutinising a sample of completed incident pro formas is a useful way of ensuring the actions against the perpetrator(s) are consistent and proportionate to the severity of incidents.

○ Rising numbers of racist incidents should be viewed positively in the first instance; it is likely that the increasing number of recorded incidents in the short term has resulted from more robust identification and recording by the school. If the pattern continues over many months, there may be underlying issues that need further investigation by the school.

○ Some schools have found 'restorative justice' approaches useful in ensuring that the same individuals do not continue to transgress. Here victim and perpetrator are brought together to unpick the deeper causes of racist behaviour. Relevant staff will need appropriate training in order to embed effective restorative-justice practice in the school.

The whole curriculum

The significance of the whole curriculum in promoting cultural diversity and race equality should not be underestimated. A curriculum that values language, culture and religion and that places the child at the centre of learning is one that will support BME/EAL learners.

The learning environment

Conducting a learning environment walk around the school each year can be an effective way to monitor the 'look and feel' of the school from the perspective of parents and children from BME backgrounds.

Here are some questions for consideration:

○ Does the main office seem welcoming to families from all ethnic backgrounds – for example, are there multilingual welcome signs, photos of pupils and adults that are representative of the local community and the pluralist nature of the UK (this is also important for schools that would describe themselves as mainly white, with fewer than 5% BME pupils)?

○ Are there dual-language/multilingual signs around the school that are commensurate with the major pupil language groups in the school?

○ Does the library stock a good range of multilingual books, bilingual dictionaries and texts that reflect a range of cultures/religions?

○ Are library books regularly audited to ensure freedom from cultural bias and/or tokenistic sentiment?

○ Are displays of work drawn from a range of pupils including beginner EAL learners?

○ Do classroom and other wall displays celebrate the multi-ethnic and multilingual nature of the school and the wider context – for example, is there a display of classwork and other initiatives with an intercultural dimension, positive role-models from a range of ethnic backgrounds, writings in other languages, and so on?

Partnership with parents

As a general rule, parents/carers of pupils from ethnic minority backgrounds are very positive about education; they will help their child with homework and support the school in its decisions. Yet some schools still find it difficult to get ethnic minority families involved in school life. For example, take-up of parents' meetings and family-learning events, as well as recruiting parent helpers, can be disappointing. While recognising the potential danger in generalising, it may be useful to consider some of the reasons why parents from some communities spurn the opportunity to become more engaged with schools.

Reasons for inconsistent parental engagement with school:

○ In some cultures teaching is left to teachers, and unless there are significant concerns parents tend to stay away from school.

○ Schools sometimes don't feel very welcoming to parents from ethnic minority backgrounds.

○ Parents/carers may worry that their level of English will be a barrier to effective communication with the school.

○ Economic circumstances may mean that both parents work, sometimes in shifts or evening work.

○ In some families the mother will not leave the home unless accompanied by an adult male – a particular issue if the father is the main bread-winner.

○ Child-care arrangement may be difficult for some families with younger siblings; they may be isolated from their community and/or not have immediate access to a family-support network such as grandparents and aunts/uncles.

Some examples of flexible working that have been shown to work with some families:

○ offering a variety of time-slots for parent meetings

○ providing interpreters where possible

○ arranging free transport to school events

○ organising childcare/crèche facilities at certain school events.

Beware ...

of the assumption that spoken fluency in a language means that a parent also possesses literacy in that language.

Using interpreters and translated materials

Using home languages as a vehicle to assist communication between school and the family is a vital strategy. Many parents will appreciate having interpreters present during meetings and will also benefit from having key

Useful translated materials

100 words in 22+ languages: http://www.school-portal. co.uk/GroupHomepage. asp?GroupID=730832

Home-school communication letters: http://www. primaryresources.co.uk/letters

Translated customisable question-and-answer booklets for parents newly arrived in the UK: http://microsites.seqfl.org. uk/view_page.php?id=601

written documents translated. However, while some parents/carers will confidently speak certain languages, some will not be able to read their first language, either because they speak a dialect that has no written form or because they never learned it in their country of origin.

Obviously, some parents/carers of EAL learners will not need interpreting/ translation services. In rare circumstances, some parents/carers will say that they feel uncomfortable with the use of their first language. They may say that they don't want their child to use their first language at school and that they intend to speak only English at home. This sort of perception needs to be gently, but firmly, challenged.

Useful points to raise with parents who resist the importance of maintaining the first language are:

- Research shows that being bilingual or multilingual conveys intellectual advantage.

- It is well established that proficiency in one language can support the development of subsequent languages; in other words, learning the first language will help the acquisition of English.

- Language is inextricably linked with culture – children and young people need to keep in touch with their own cultural roots while adjusting to British culture, else they may become caught between cultures, unclear about their real identity.

- When learning a new language, it is important to have periods of time out as it may be very tiring. Engaging in activities in a language in which they are more proficient is perfect for this.

- While speaking only in English at home may seem a good idea, in some families parents/carers may be modelling insecure use of English that may serve to be more confusing than helpful.

Useful resource

http://www.cilt.org.uk/ community_languages/valuing_ community_languages.aspx

Family learning

Many schools find opportunities to involve parents with their children through family learning. Here are some examples of events that have been highly successful:

- 'how schools work' courses – explaining all about the UK education system

- developing reading skills through home languages

- workshops explaining how to support children at home

- e-safety workshops – safe use of the internet and social networking sites

- explaining about the exam system – parents try out sample test questions

- showing parents how different subjects are taught – see case study on p. 68.

Useful resources

Developing reading skills through home languages (2008) London Borough of Redbridge EMA Team, Melbourne Road, Ilford, Essex, IG1 4HT

Know it all – e-safety with multilingual translation: http://www.childnet-int.org/ kia/parents

Mathematics family-learning workshop

In one school, a parental survey about homework identified specific issues for parents who had been educated abroad. In particular, some parents felt insecure about supporting their children's learning of mathematics. The school targeted a number of parents, inviting them by letter to attend a series of workshops; letters were translated where appropriate. This initial invitation was followed up with a phone call by a bilingual practitioner. The five sessions were organised as shown.

Session(s)	Content	Support	Who?
1	Introduction to the UK mathematics curriculum	Teacher and bilingual practitioners	Parents
2	Techniques for solving mathematical number problems	Teacher and bilingual practitioners	Parents
3 & 4	Practical workshops on number problems	Teacher and bilingual practitioners	Parents and pupils
5	Sharing different numerical methods from around the world	Teacher and bilingual practitioners	Parents

Parents were very positive about the experience, reporting a variety of benefits – including raised levels of confidence and better understanding of current mathematics teaching methods. However, there were some surprising benefits for the school. Most interestingly, school staff became more familiar with different ways of solving number problems from around the world and were able to incorporate the ideas into their teaching.

Resources

More information about Hampshire Ethnic Minority and Traveller Achievement Service's 'Young Interpreter scheme' may be found at: http://www3.hants.gov.uk/education/ema/ema-schools/ema-good-practice/ema-pupil-interpreters.htm

Using pupils as a resource

There is tremendous potential within the school community for both bilingual and monolingual pupils to be able to use their linguistic and social skills to support their EAL peers and contribute to the wider agenda of promoting linguistic and cultural diversity. Different schemes have been shown to work, such as peer buddying, young interpreters (as developed by Hampshire Ethnic Minority and Traveller Achievement Service – see case study opposite) and mentoring of younger pupils by older learners.

Case study

Young interpreters' scheme

Farzan, a Year-6 pupil, has been trained as a 'young interpreter' in her school. Part of her working week is described in a diary extract.

Monday a.m.

Mrs Jones asked me to show a family around the school this morning. I was able to speak to them in my language which I think helped a lot. I think I will be buddying their daughter Nazmun. She seemed nice.

Monday lunchtime

Sally and I sat with Pedro at lunchtime while we ate our lunch. We couldn't speak to him as we don't speak Spanish, but we had a laugh trying to teach him some new English words. It was fun! He taught us some Spanish words as well like 'hola', which means hello. *[Pedro is a Year-4 new-arrival pupil]*

Tuesday lunchtime

Pedro and I read 'Buri and the Marrow'. He read it in Spanish and then I listened to him reading in English. He did really well.

Wednesday

Nazmun started school today. She is in my class and I sat next to her all day. We were able to talk in Bengali when she didn't understand what was going on. Actually she can speak some English but said she felt self-conscious about talking in English at the moment. Before home-time Nazmun mentioned that when she was in the toilets, a girl had kicked her for no reason. I told Mrs Jones about it.

During language club this afternoon, I taught everyone the colours and numbers in Bengali as well as how to greet someone with 'Asalaam Alaykum' We are going to learn some Nepali next week.

The above scenario illustrates some of the more common activities that pupils can be involved with:

- ● showing pupils and parents around the school
- ● acting as a buddy for new arrivals
- ● using ability in their first language to communicate with peers and act as a school interpreter where appropriate
- ● helping new-arrival pupils in curriculum time
- ● supporting the integration of EAL learners informally by offering language taster sessions for pupils and staff.

It is essential that pupils undertake comprehensive training in order to be fully prepared for the different types of role that they may be required to fulfil. Pupils should be recognised appropriately for their efforts.

Links beyond the school

Here are some questions for consideration:

○ Has the school created school links locally and/or nationally to foster community cohesion initiatives?

○ Have international links been developed – for example, with schools in countries representative of the black and ethnic minority / EAL pupil population or between multi-ethnic schools abroad and mainly white UK schools ?

○ Are staff aware of local language schools and does the school celebrate the first-language achievements of its EAL learners?

○ Does the school make use of local community and religious centres – for example, for educational visits?

○ Are visiting speakers drawn from BME backgrounds to act as positive role-models – for example, from public services and the world of sport and entertainment?

○ Is the school curriculum enriched by visiting experts – for example, by developing intercultural and multilingual approaches to art, music, literature, and so on?

Case study

FlashMeeting to support isolated EAL learners

Hamid arrived at school in October 2008 and joined a Year-5 class. He was born in Afghanistan, and his family was from an asylum-seeking background. The school had very few pupils from an ethnic minority background and had never had a Pashto speaker before. Hamid had missed a lot of schooling and he spoke very little English, which presented some challenges for the school.

The school heard about a FlashMeeting video-conferencing programme from the local authority's EMAS. Using a simple web camera, microphone and internet connection, at various prearranged times Hamid was able to converse in his first language with another Pashto speaker in a different school. The benefits for Hamid were huge. He was able to ask all the questions about school that had been worrying him, he felt he had made a new friend and he understood that his language was being valued.

Linking isolated learners via FlashMeeting will require some initial preparation, including thinking about:
* informing parents about the aims of the FlashMeeting sessions
* where to locate the equipment
* when and how frequently to run meetings
* whom to link together – for example, considering age and gender issues
* how to monitor what happens in each session.

Supporting isolated EAL learners using FlashMeeting, a free video-conferencing system: http:// flashmeeting.e2bn.net

Final thoughts

For many of us it is hard to imagine what it must be like to work and function using a language in which we are not totally proficient. This book has offered an insight into the many challenges that may confront an EAL learner, whether a complete beginner or a more advanced learner. The guidance about effective provision for EAL learners has been informed by over 25 years of research and is intended to be both practical and flexible.

One of the key messages is that EAL learners have individual needs and that, while quality-first teaching will be of benefit to all learners, there is something distinctive about teaching and learning for pupils learning EAL.

As a last thought I present a list of my top ten considerations. Practitioners need to:

- ensure that BME/EAL learners are safe from discrimination in all its guises

- develop work that builds upon the knowledge and skills that EAL learners bring with them from their previous educational/cultural/religious background

- appreciate that EAL learners are language enabled, not language deficient – they will have proficiency in one or more languages that will support their development of English

- understand that most EAL learners do not have SEN, although some do

- teach inclusively – the mainstream classroom is the most appropriate learning environment for the majority of EAL learners

- group EAL learners according to cognitive ability, not level of proficiency in English

- recognise that some EAL learners will require specific intervention for speaking, listening, reading and writing

- plan collaborative work in which talk is central to learning

- consider the language demands of tasks across the curriculum and plan specific strategies to address them

- utilise the expertise of other adults, including TAs, bilingual practitioners and parents.

References

Blair, M. and J. Bourne (1998) Making the difference: teaching and learning strategies in successful multi-ethnic schools: http://www.dcsf.gov.uk/research/data/uploadfiles/RB59.pdf

Cameron, L. and S. Besser (2004) Writing in English as an additional language at Key Stage 2, DfES RR586: http://www.dcsf.gov.uk/research/data/uploadfiles/RR586.pdf

Cummins, J. (1979) Cognitive/academic language proficiency, linguistic interdependence, the optimum age question and some other matters, *Working Papers on Bilingualism*, No. 19, 121–129

Cummins, J. (1984) *Bilingualism and Special Education: Issues in Assessment and Pedagogy*, Clevedon, England: Multilingual Matters

DfES (2007) Pupil Language Data: Supplementary guidance for local authorities on schools' collection and recording of data on pupils' languages

Hall, D., D. Griffiths, L. Haslam and Y. Wilson (2001) *Assessing the Needs of Bilingual Pupils*, London: David Fulton Publishers

Krashen, S. (1981) *Second Language Acquisition and Second Language Learning*, Oxford: Pergamon

Thomas, W.P. and V. Collier (1997) *School Effectiveness for Language Minority Students*, Washington DC: National Clearinghouse for Bilingual Education

Vygotsky, L.S. (1962) *Thought and Language*, Cambridge, MA: MIT Press

Wegerif, R. (2004) The role of ICT as catalyst and support for dialogue, *NALDIC Quarterly*, vol. 1, no. 4